Easy-to-Make Costumes

9.95   NE

W9-DBK-768

DATE DUE

EASY-TO-MAKE COSTUMES

by Kathryn Harrison and Valerie Kohn

a Sterling/Tamos book

1992

Library of Congress Cataloging-in-Publication Data

Harrison, Kathryn.
  Easy-to-make costumes / by Kathryn Harrison and Valerie Kohn
      p.   cm.
  "A Sterling/Tamos book."
  Includes index.
  ISBN 1-895569-00-1
  1. Costume. 2. Handicraft. I. Kohn, Valerie. II. Title.
TT633.H37 1992
646.4'78 — dc20   91–33587
                                  CIP

Canadian Cataloguing in Publication Data

Harrison, Kathryn, 1952-
  Easy-to-make costumes

  "A Sterling/Tamos book"
  ISBN 1-895569-00-1

1. Children - Costume. 2. Dressmaking - Patterns.
3. Children's clothing. I. Kohn, Valerie, 1950-.
II. Title.

TT633.H277 1992   646/.478   C91–097153-6

A Sterling / Tamos Book
First paperback edition published 1993
© 1992 by Kathryn Harrison and Valerie Kohn

Sterling Publishing Company, Inc.
387 Park Avenue South, New York, NY 10016

Tamos Press Limited
300 Wales Avenue, Winnipeg, MB, Canada R2M 2S9

10 9 8 7 6 5 4 3 2 1

Distributed in Canada by Sterling Publishing
c/o Canadian Manda Group, P.O. Box 920, Station U
Toronto, Ontario, Canada M8Z 5P9
Distributed in Great Britain and Europe by Cassell PLC
Villiers House, 41/47 Strand, London WC2N 5JE, England
Distributed in Australia by Capricorn Link Ltd.
P.O. Box 665, Lane Cove, NSW 2066

Illustrations and paper projects created by Teddy Cameron Long
Fabric projects created by Claudia Kopczewski
Design by A. O. Osen
Photography by Doug Ritter

Sterling ISBN 1-895569-00-1 Trade
            1-895569-10-9 Paper

The advice and directions given in this book have been carefully checked, prior to printing, by the Authors as well as the Publisher. Nevertheless, no guarantee can be given as to project outcome due to possible differences in material and the Authors and Publisher will not be responsible for the results.

TABLE OF CONTENTS

INTRODUCTION

How many times have you been asked to make a costume for your child? It's Halloween. There's a Christmas pageant. Your child is in a school play or a community center project. Whatever the occasion the circumstances always seem to be the same. There isn't enough time to plan an elaborate costume and you can't buy one because your child wants something different or he/she needs a particular outfit to suit a special event.

The costumes in this book are designed to help you deal with these situations. The forty-three different costumes not only look wonderful, but they're inexpensive and simple to make. You can use up pieces of left-over material and add purchased accessories to create the best looking spanish dancer, or ask your grocer for leftover cardboard boxes for a jack-in-the-box, or buy a bit of fake fur for a bunny suit, or cardboard for a pizza costume. Your child will be proud to wear any of these designs.

Some of the costume subjects are traditional, others are unusual. You've probably seen many little witches and ghosts out "Trick or Treating" on Halloween but it's unlikely you've ever seen a chocolate chip cookie or a bucket of paint walking around. Children love the novelty, and they can even help make the costumes. When it's a family activity the children feel a real sense of accomplishment and they enjoy the admiration of their friends.

Don't worry if your art skills aren't well developed. The basic instructions are easy to follow and as you go along you may wish to add your own finishing touches for a particular look. You'll be surprised how creative you can be. These are fun projects that don't require skilled makers. If you sew a seam that isn't straight or have two sides of cardboard that overlap at the wrong place, an extra pom-pom or a bit of braid or some paint will usually cover up the errors.

The projects require a minimum of materials—some cardboard, glue, paint, pieces of fabric, a needle and thread. You can add extra bows or trim from pieces you have around the house or buy a bit of glitter or lace to make the costume special. The finished costumes are inexpensive and you'll be pleased that your child has a great looking outfit that's exactly right for the occasion.

GENERAL DIRECTIONS

Sizes are not given in absolutes because children come in all sizes, so, by all means, make adjustments as necessary. Patterns for sewn costumes are approximately size 6. Follow the directions to enlarge or make smaller on the next page.

Substitutions are always possible. If the directions call for coloring with a felt-tipped marker but you would find it easier to spray paint or use self-adhesive paper—go ahead!

Some of the materials are called for frequently. Cardboard (rippled on one side or smooth on both sides) is available where you purchase children's art supplies—department stores, large drug stores, etc. Cardboard circles can be found wherever cake decorating supplies are sold. The circles come in a variety of sizes. Double-faced tape and poster paint can be purchased in hardware, craft, and department stores; yarn at department stores or wool stores; fabrics, lace, ribbon, thread at fabric stores; feathers and flowers at a large artificial flower store; and glitter, face paint, and novelties at a party store.

Have fun! Most of these directions can be altered with some imagination. You may create something we didn't think of. Once you begin, anything is possible.

Sample pattern

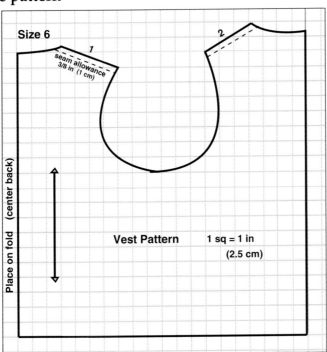

Size 6

1

seam allowance
3/8 in (1 cm)

2

Place on fold   (center back)

Vest Pattern   1 sq = 1 in
(2.5 cm)

Each square represents 1 in (2.5 cm). To make pattern larger or smaller, enlarge or decrease the size of the squares. For example, if you want a size twice as large as the diagram make the squares twice as large. Reverse the procedure to make a smaller size. With a pencil, ruler, and large piece of paper, draw a smaller or larger grid using the size of square you need. Copy the pattern diagram onto the new grid a square at a time. Cut out the new pattern. Place on fabric and cut out.

Equipment used

 5-minute epoxy glue

 Awl

 Cellophane tape

 Felt marker

 Masking tape

 Paint brush

Pencil

Ruler

Scissors

Stapler

Utility Knife

White glue

Wire cutter

Making actual pattern

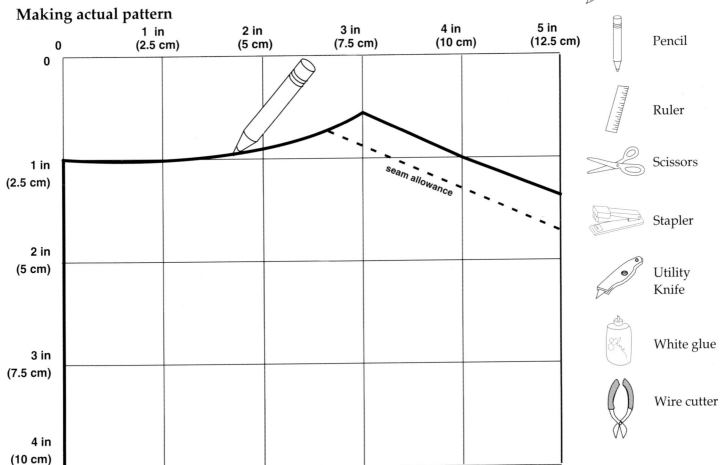

0

1 in
(2.5 cm)

2 in
(5 cm)

3 in
(7.5 cm)

4 in
(10 cm)

5 in
(12.5 cm)

0

1 in
(2.5 cm)

2 in
(5 cm)

3 in
(7.5 cm)

4 in
(10 cm)

seam allowance

BASIC TECHNIQUES

The 43 costumes in this book are all easy to make and most can be constructed using one of these simple basic techniques. Each technique has been given a letter (A, B, C, D, E, F, G, or H) and is outlined step-by-step on the following pages. The letter that corresponds to the required technique is shown beside the appropriate costume throughout the book. Techniques involve cutting, gluing, and taping cardboard or foam; sewing cloth; or making papier-mâché. Where no letter is given beside a costume the complete instructions are included with that particular costume.

A Basic Cylinder Technique
B Basic Sandwich Board Technique
C Basic Box Technique
D Basic Tunic Technique
E Basic Vest Technique
F Basic Bowl Hat
G Basic Cylinder Hat
H Basic Cone Hat

A Basic Cylinder

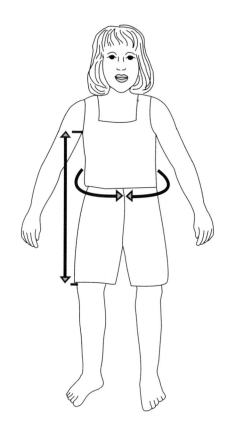

DIRECTIONS FOR BASIC TECHNIQUE

Cylinders may be made with the rippled cardboard on the outside or the inside, depending on the effect desired.

Materials
1 sheet of corrugated cardboard, one side rippled
double-faced tape (or glue)
2-in (5-cm) -wide ribbon— 2 pieces, each 24 in (61 cm) long

1. Lay cardboard flat. Measure around body of child, allowing room for clothing. Transfer this measurement onto the cardboard, across ripples, as shown (a), and cut. Measure from underarm to knee of child. This is the length needed. Mark this length on cardboard and cut (b).

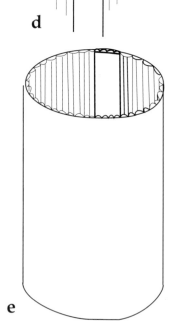

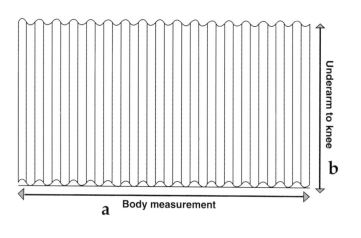

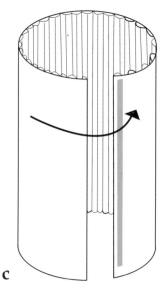

2. Secure double-faced tape from top to bottom along short edge of cardboard. Remove backing from other side of tape. Secure this side of double-faced tape (c) to opposite short end of cardboard, overlap as shown.

3. Alternative method for closing: Cut additional length of cardboard 3 ridges wide and as long as the project. Glue ridged side and place over butted ends of cardboard sheet so that ridges fit together smoothly (d), (e).

4. Cut out a small square 4 in by 4 in (10 cm by 10 cm) under each armpit to make the fit more comfortable (f). Some costumes require a hole cut out for arms, as shown (g).

5. Using a sharp object, poke 2 pairs of holes in the front and 2 pairs of holes in the back of the cylinder, each pair 1 in (2.5 cm) apart (h).

6. Insert one piece of ribbon into one front hole entering from the inside. Push ribbon through paired hole and knot on the inside of the cylinder. Repeat with other front hole and second piece of ribbon (h).

7. Put the costume on. Draw ribbons over the child's shoulders and cross at back (i). Poke the other ends of the ribbons through each hole. Adjust costume to position desired. Secure each ribbon with a knot on the inside of the cylinder. Cut off excess ribbon.

8. If the child will be sitting in this costume, cut out a half oval shape at the back of the cylinder from the hip level, as shown (j).

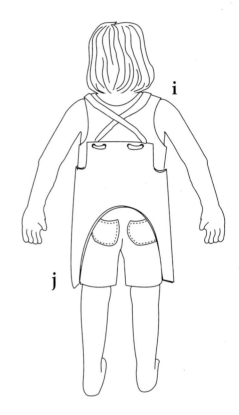

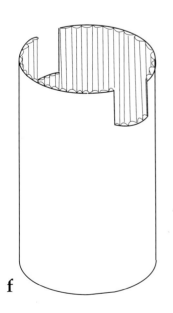

f

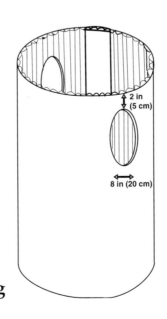

g

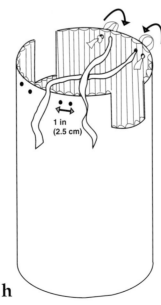

h

Basic Cylinder A 9

B Basic Sandwich Board

DIRECTIONS FOR BASIC TECHNIQUE

Materials
2 pieces smooth stiff cardboard
2-in (5-cm) -wide ribbon —2 pieces,
** each 18 in (46 cm) long**

1. Cut each cardboard piece to the shape required (square, circle, etc.) for the front and back of the costume (a). A circle 24 in (61 cm) in diameter will fit a child 4 to 8 years old. Each piece should be identical in shape and size. Paint suitable to the project.

2. Poke 2 pairs of holes in the front cardboard piece about 4 in (10 cm) from each outside edge. Make paired holes 1 in (2.5 cm) from each other, as shown (b). Do the same for the back piece.

3. Insert one piece of ribbon into one front hole, entering from the inside. Push ribbon back through paired hole and knot on the inside of the board. Repeat with other front hole and second piece of ribbon.

4. Put the costume on (c). Draw ribbons over child's shoulders and cross at the back. Poke the other ends of the ribbons through the holes in the back board, in the same way. Adjust lengths. Knot on inside of board (b). Clip off excess ribbon and secure with glue or tape.

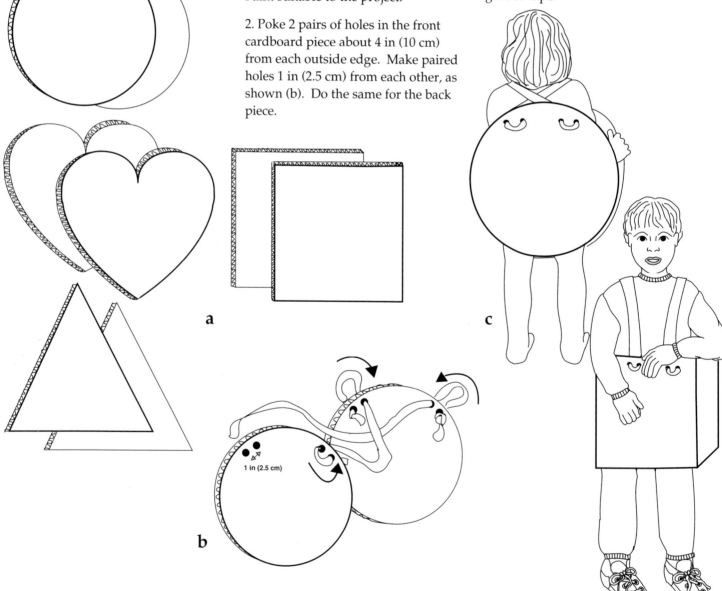

a

b

1 in (2.5 cm)

c

C Basic Box

DIRECTIONS FOR BASIC TECHNIQUE

Materials

One square cardboard box—choose size to fit your child

2-in (5-cm) -wide ribbon—2 pieces, each 24 in (61 cm) long

1. Cut top and bottom flaps from the box (a).

2. Box is low enough on body so that armholes are not required (b)

3. Using a sharp object, poke 2 pairs of holes in the front and 2 pairs of holes in the back of the box about 4 in (10 cm) from each outside edge. Paired holes are l in (2.5 cm) apart (c).

4. Insert one piece of ribbon into one front hole, entering from the inside. Push ribbon back through paired hole and knot on the inside of the box. Repeat with other front hole and second piece of ribbon (d).

5. Put the costume on. Draw ribbons over child's shoulders and cross at the back. Poke the other ends of the ribbons through the holes in back of the box in the same way. Adjust length and knot on inside of box. Clip off excess ribbon and secure with glue or tape.

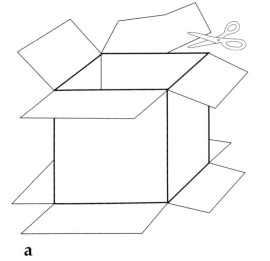

a

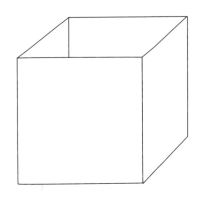

b

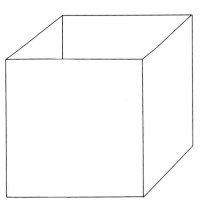

c

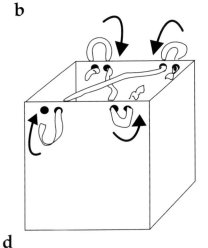

d

SEWING TIPS

When choosing fabric for your costume select materials that do not fray easily. This will eliminate extra hand work on seams and hems. Fabrics that show signs of fraying or unraveling can be zigzagged by a conventional sewing machine or serged if you have an overlock machine.

Where possible apply decorations such as lace, braid, or other trims while the fabric can still lie flat, i.e. before gathering or sewing seams together. This will eliminate extra hand work.

When using velcro for fasteners place the scratchy piece on the bottom opening and the soft piece on the top opening to lap over the bottom velcro. In this way if the closure doesn't overlap exactly, the soft velcro will touch the child's skin and still be comfortable to wear.

Narrow trims are easier to manage if you are a novice seamstress.

If applying more than one lace or trim to a garment that is gathered, apply the lace to widest area of fabric first, working towards the narrowest area.

Lace can be purchased already gathered and is much easier to handle.

Basic Tunic

Pattern

Note: Pattern given is for size 6. Each square represents 1 in (2.5 cm). To make pattern larger or smaller, enlarge or decrease the size of the squares. For example, if you want a size twice as large as the diagram make the squares twice as large. Reverse the procedure to make a smaller design. With a pencil, ruler, and large piece of paper, draw a smaller or larger grid using the size of square you need. Copy the pattern diagram onto the new grid a square at a time. Cut out the new pattern. Place on fabric and cut out.

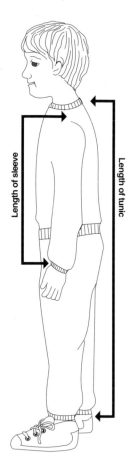

a

DIRECTIONS FOR BASIC TECHNIQUE

Materials

2 lengths plus length of sleeve of fabric of your choice. Measure length of tunic your child needs (a).
velcro for closures
elastic for full sleeve
bias tape (optional)

To Make Basic Tunic

1. Lay pattern pieces on your fabric placing pieces along folds, as indicated (b), and cut pieces out.

2. Stitch velcro to each side of neck opening so that velcro secures opening when sides are brought together (c).

3. Stitch the sleeve dart together (1, 2) on the inside of fabric. Press open. Basic tunic has tapered sleeve.

4. Stitch front sleeves to front tunic and stitch back sleeves to back tunic (d).

5. Stitch underarm and side seams. Press all seams flat.

6. Turn under neck hem and stitch.

7. Turn under hems on sleeves and tunic bottom and stitch.

Variation

If a fuller costume is desired make this variation.

1. Use the tunic pattern and add 2 in (5 cm) to the center front and back widths. Place on fold. Eliminate the velcro opening slit.

2. Make a casing at the neck edge (do not hem neck) for an elastic or drawstring. (See instructions below.)

3. If full sleeves are used, make a casing at the hem for elastic. Sleeves may also hang loose if costume requires this look.

To Make Casing

1. Sew one side of 1 in (2.5 cm) unfolded bias tape to neck edge or sleeve edge on right side of fabric (e).

2. Turn under and stitch down on wrong side of fabric, leaving small opening to insert elastic (f).

3. Thread elastic through casing. Measure size you need and cut off elastic end (g). Sew elastic ends together. Sew opening closed (h).

To Make Suit With Legs

1. Using basic tunic pattern cut out leg areas and suit pieces as indicated for bunny suit. You will have 2 back and 2 front pieces. Sew back seam. Turn under seam allowance for neck opening and stitch.

2. Sew 3 velcro closures to each side of long neck opening at the back to close suit, as shown in (b) and (c).

3. Stitch seams.

4. For bunny suit it is not necessary to hem neck, sleeves, and legs.

To Make A Blouse

1. Use basic tunic pattern and cut off where indicated on the pattern (b).

2. Stitch together same as for tunic.

NOTE: Patterns given are for North American size 6 child. However, patterns are generous and allow for extra roominess to fit over child's clothes.

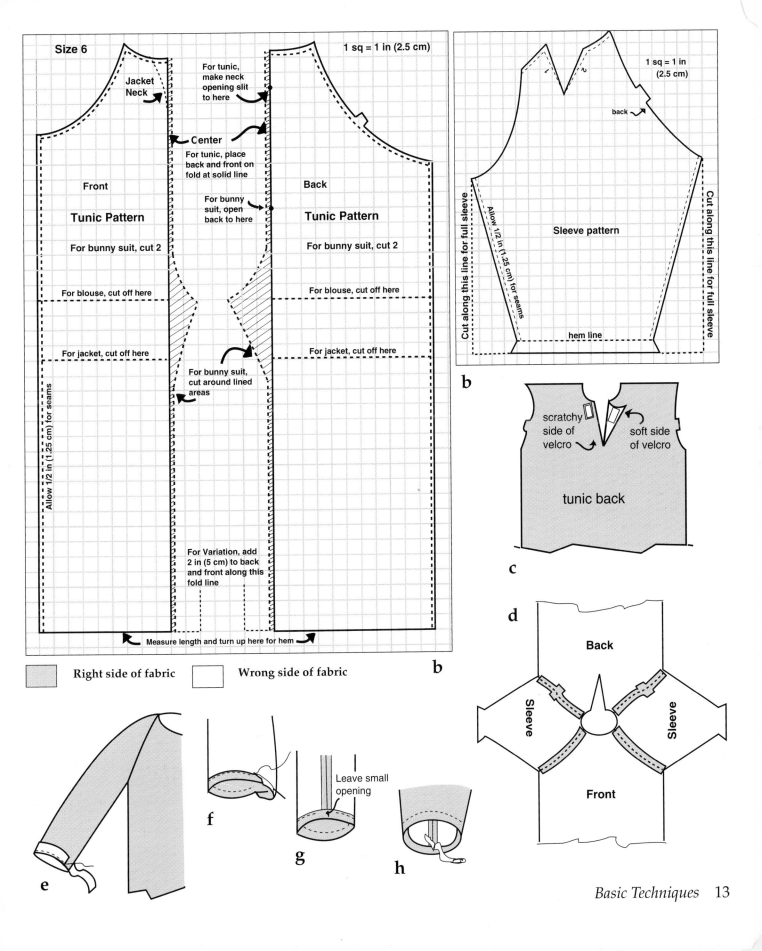

Size 6

Jacket Neck

For tunic, make neck opening slit to here

Center

For tunic, place back and front on fold at solid line

For bunny suit, open back to here

1 sq = 1 in (2.5 cm)

Front

Tunic Pattern

For bunny suit, cut 2

Back

Tunic Pattern

For bunny suit, cut 2

For blouse, cut off here

For blouse, cut off here

For jacket, cut off here

For jacket, cut off here

For bunny suit, cut around lined areas

Allow 1/2 in (1.25 cm) for seams

For Variation, add 2 in (5 cm) to back and front along this fold line

Measure length and turn up here for hem

Right side of fabric   Wrong side of fabric

b

1 sq = 1 in (2.5 cm)

back

Cut along this line for full sleeve

Cut along this line for full sleeve

Allow 1/2 in (1.25 cm) for seams

Sleeve pattern

hem line

b

scratchy side of velcro   soft side of velcro

tunic back

c

d

Back

Sleeve   **Sleeve**

Front

e

f

g   Leave small opening

h

Basic Techniques 13

E Basic Vest

Materials
fabric of your choice
velcro or purchased fasteners for closures
bias tape or ribbon binding

To Make Vest (long or short)

1. Stitch shoulder seams together on inside, matching 1, 2 (a). Try vest on child and adjust the fit. Gather at sides if needed.

2. Turn under hem allowance on neck, armholes, fronts, and bottom, and stitch , or use tape or ribbon binding.

3. Turn under hem allowance on fronts and stitch. Vest can be worn open. If vest is to be closed, sew velcro to each side front, or sew on fasteners (b).

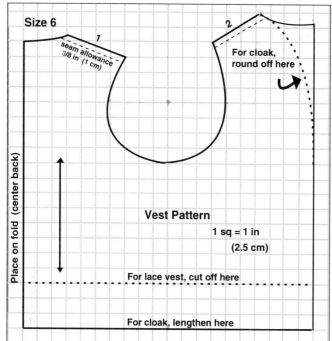

Size 6

1

seam allowance
3/8 in (1 cm)

2

For cloak, round off here

Place on fold (center back)

Vest Pattern

1 sq = 1 in
(2.5 cm)

For lace vest, cut off here

For cloak, lengthen here

a

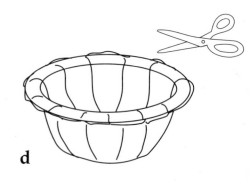

b

F Basic Bowl Hat

1. Place the bowl in a plastic bag. Turn the bowl upside down on a protected work surface, and smooth the plastic down over the bowl (a).

2. Wet a sheet of newspaper with water, lay it over the bowl and smooth in place (b). Spread glue over the newspaper (b).

3. Repeat, alternating newspaper and glue until you have 6 layers (c). Leave in warm place to dry overnight.

4. When dry, remove the paper from the bowl, and trim edges with scissors (d).

5. Paint or decorate.

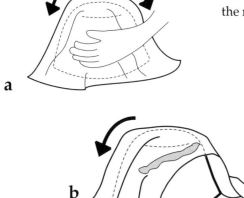

a

b

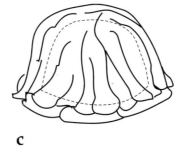

c

d

G Basic Cylinder Hat

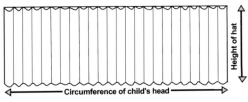

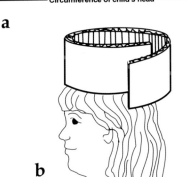

a

b

1. Cut a strip of rippled cardboard across the ripples long enough to go around the child's head and as wide as you wish the hat to be high (a).

2. Wrap the strip around the child's head to determine the exact size (b). Cut off the excess cardboard and tape or glue the ends together the same way as for basic body cylinder, see p 8 .

3. To make lid top draw a circle on a piece of smooth cardboard, slightly larger than the hat circle. Cut out (c).

4. Spread glue over the top edges of the hat cylinder (d).

5. Press the cardboard circle onto the glue. Tape in place until the glue dries (e).

6. Decorate to suit costume you are making.

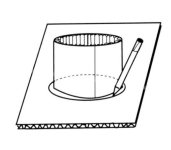

c

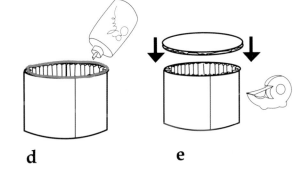

d

e

H Basic Cone Hat

1. Cut a sheet of heavy paper into a 24 in (61 cm) square (a).

2. Starting one-quarter up one side, roll into a cone shape, as shown (b). Adjust to fit child's head.

3. Tape cone, as shown (c), or glue overlapped edges.

4. Trim edges evenly so cone hat fits head (c).

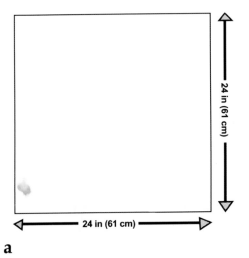

a

b

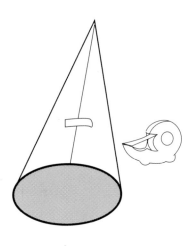

c

Dice

1. **Make 2 Basic Boxes C** p 11.

2. Cover the prepared boxes with white paper or paint the outside surfaces white (a).

3. Cut out 14 circles, 3 in (7.5 cm) in diameter from black paper (b) for each die.

4. Glue 14 circles on the sides of each box to resemble each die (c).
Remember opposite sides must add up to seven.

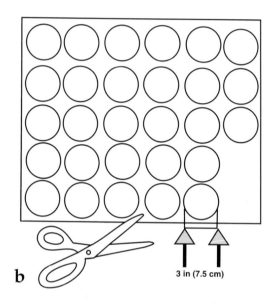

b

3 in (7.5 cm)

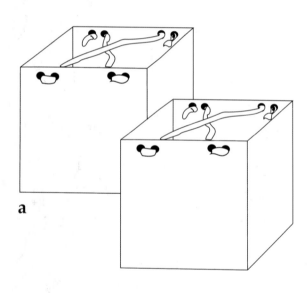

a

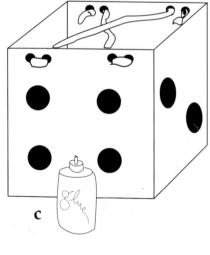

c

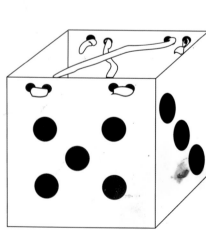

A&G

Pickle Jar

1. **Make Basic Cylinder A** p 8. Be sure the smooth side of the cardboard faces outward (a).

2. Paint the cylinder to resemble a jar of pickles (see photograph).

3. **Make Basic Cylinder Hat G** p 15.

4. Cut a large circle, 20 in (51 cm) in diameter using smooth cardboard, for the top of the hat (b) .

5. Cut a long strip of cardboard across the ripples, 2 in (5 cm) wide, to fit around circle (c). Glue the edge of this strip around the rim of the large circle, as shown (d).

6. Glue the circle to the hat cylinder so that the rim hangs down (e).

7. Paint to resemble a pickle jar lid.

8. Ribbons can be attached at sides to hold lid more securely. Paint the child's face green if desired.

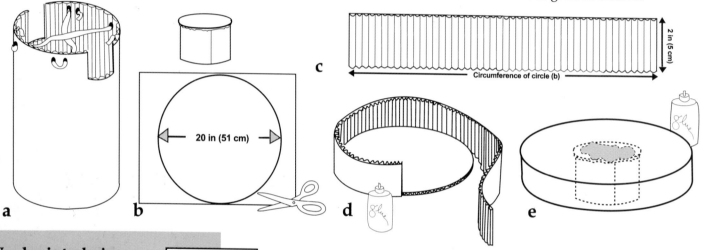

a

b

20 in (51 cm)

c

Circumference of circle (b)

2 in (5 cm)

d

e

B

Pizza

1. **Make Basic Sandwich Board B** p 10 using 2 large circles 30 in (76 cm) in diameter.

2. Cut many long curved strips of cardboard about 1 in (2.5 cm) wide and glue these around the edges of the front board, as shown (a). Trim the edges to resemble the crust.

3. From cardboard scraps, cut out many small circles 2 in (5 cm) in diameter (b). Cut out more scraps 2 in (5 cm) long and 1/2 in (1 cm) wide. Cut out many mushroom shapes

2 in (5 cm) high. Glue all of these on the front board.

4 . Paint the front sandwich board a creamy yellow to resemble mozzarella cheese. Paint the "crust" a darker yellow-brown. The back board can also be painted this color.

5. Paint the small circles a dull red-brown to resemble pepperoni, the rectangular scraps green for green pepper, and the mushroom shapes a greyish-brown.

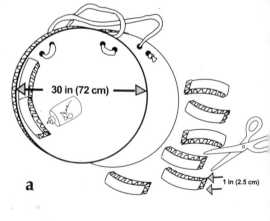

30 in (72 cm)

a

1 in (2.5 cm)

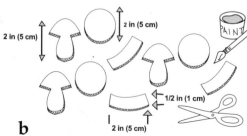

2 in (5 cm)

2 in (5 cm)

PAINT

1/2 in (1 cm)

2 in (5 cm)

b

Root Beer Mug

A

1. **Make Basic Cylinder A** p 8 with armholes. Be sure the smooth side of the cardboard faces outward. This is the body of the mug (a).

To Make Handle

1. Draw a handle shape 4 in (10 cm) wide, as shown (b) on smooth firm cardboard. Make sure the height of the handle is less than the height of the body cylinder.

2. Cut out the handle. Make a second identical handle shape and cut it out .

3. Cut a length of rippled cardboard 6 in (15 cm) wide and long enough to fit around the outside curve of the handle. Cut the length **across** the ripples, as shown (c).

4. Lay the cardboard strip flat, rippled side up. Place a measuring stick on the strip along the long edge, 1 in (2.5 cm) from the edge. Draw a sharp knife along the ruler, scoring the ripples but not cutting completely through the cardboard, as shown (d).

5. Pull off the rippled layer of paper along the outer edges, leaving the flat layer of paper beneath it, as shown (e). Repeat this procedure on the other side of the cardboard strip.

6. Make 1 in (2.5 cm) cuts along the flat strips of paper all along both sides of the long rippled strip, as shown (f).

7. Spread glue along the flat strips of paper on one side of the center rippled strip (g).

8. Place the outside curve of the handle shape on the paper so that the side of the handle is against the cut edges of the ripples, as shown (h).

9. Fold the flat glued strip of paper over and onto the handle shape, as shown (i). Tape in place if necessary.

10. Repeat this procedure on the other side of the rippled strip with the

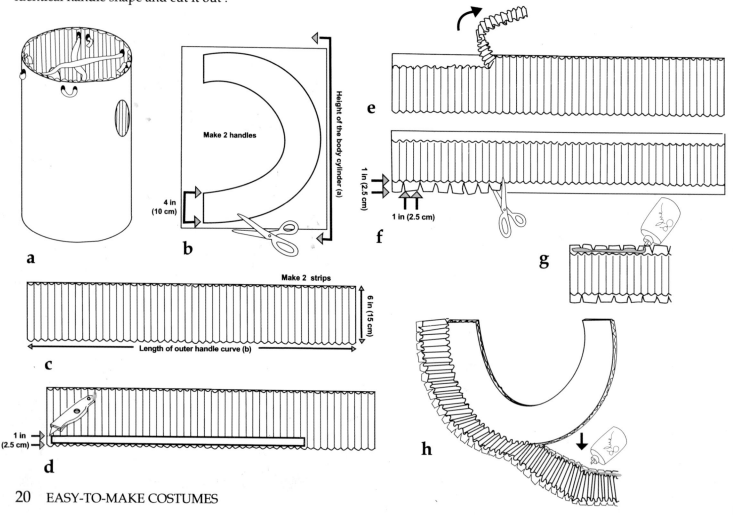

Make 2 handles

4 in (10 cm)

Height of the body cylinder (a)

1 in (2.5 cm)

1 in (2.5 cm)

a

b

e

f

g

Make 2 strips

Length of outer handle curve (b)

6 in (15 cm)

c

1 in (2.5 cm)

d

h

Root Beer Mug continued.
second handle shape (j).

11. Cut another rippled strip of cardboard long and wide enough to fit around the inside edge of the handle and across the ends. Remove 1 in (2.5 cm) from each side, as before.

12. Glue this second piece to one end of the handle and continue around the inside curve of the handle, as shown (k). Tape in place if necessary.

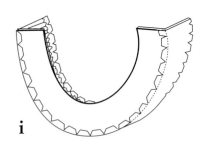

i

13. When the glue is dry, attach the handle to the back of the body cylinder with glue. Hold in place with tape until dry (l).

14. Paint to resemble a root beer mug. Paint the top 4 in (10 cm) and the bottom 4 in (10 cm) of the cylinder grey to resemble frosted glass (l).

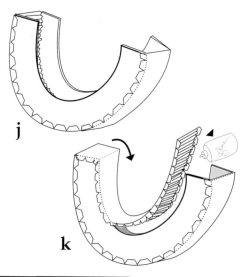

j

k

Paint the center of the mug dark brown.

15. Glue polyester stuffing around the top of the body cylinder. Arrange it to resemble the foam on top of a root beer mug, as shown (l). Child can wear additional stuffing on top of the head as a hat if desired.

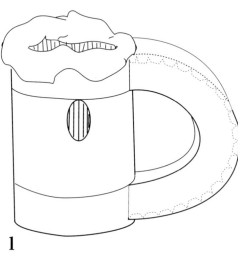

l

Use basic techniques

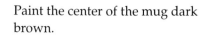

Popcorn Tub

1. **Make Basic Cylinder A** p 8 but do not cut places for arms. Be sure the smooth side of the cardboard faces outward (a).

2. Paint the cylinder to resemble a cardboard tub of popcorn.

3. With a strong glue, attach styrofoam packing chips to the top edge of the cylinder, as shown (b). Dab yellow paint on the styrofoam chips to resemble butter.

To Make Hat

1. **Make Basic Bowl Hat F** p 14 (c) with no brim.

2. Glue styrofoam packing chips all over the paper bowl hat (d).

3. Dab yellow paint on the styrofoam chips to resemble butter (d).

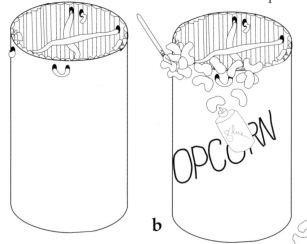

a   b

c

d

Lamb

Materials
cotton batting
double-faced tape
Costume is assembled on a white track suit.

1. Roll bulk cotton batting into a number of small balls.

2. For the lamb's wool, attach the balls to the track suit using either double-faced tape, glue, or needle and thread (a).

To Make Lamb's Feet

1. Draw a hoof shape on cardboard 5 in (12.5 cm) long and 3 in (7.5 cm) wide and cut out. Make 4 hooves in this manner (b).

2. Paint black.

3. Poke 2 holes in the base of each hoof and thread a piece of yarn or ribbon, long enough to tie each hoof to child's wrist or ankle, through the holes, as shown (c).

To Make Lamb's Ears

1. Draw 2 ear shapes on smooth cardboard 4 in (10 cm) long and 2 in (5 cm) wide (d). Cut out , paint black.

2. On rippled cardboard draw an oval 6 in (15 cm) long and 3 in (7.5 cm) wide. Cut out (e).

3. Punch 1 hole in each end of rippled cardboard (f).

4. Cut 2 pieces of ribbon, long enough to tie under child's chin, and thread through holes in end of rippled cardboard oval (g). Knot on smooth side.

5. Glue ears to ends over top of holes.

6. Spread glue over smooth cardboard and attach cotton balls (h).

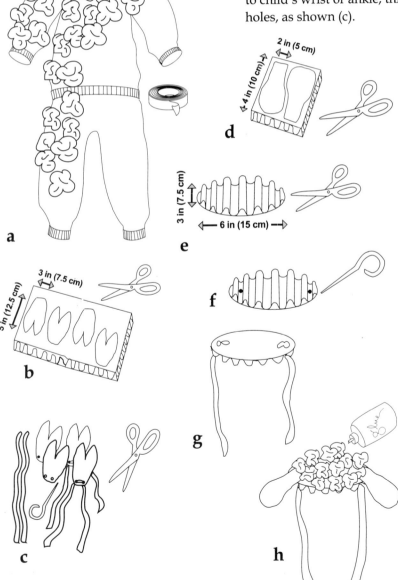

Paint Can

A&G

1. **Make Basic Cylinder A** with arm holes p 8. Make sure the smooth side of the cardboard faces outward (a).

2. Glue a 4-in (10-cm) -wide strip of aluminum foil around the top and bottom edges of the cylinder, as shown (b).

3. Paint the center of the cylinder to resemble a paint can label. Use the color name "Sea Blue."

4. Unbend a coat hanger for a handle (c). Cut off ends with wire cutters. Cover the ends with tape and tape to each side of the cylinder so that the handle hangs down in the front (d).

To Make Hat

1. **Make Basic Cylinder Hat G** p 15.

2. Cut two circles 18 in (45 cm) in diameter from cardboard. On one circle measure in 1 in (2.5 cm) around circle and cut out inner circle. Glue 2 large circles together. Cut out 1 circle (from discarded circle) 9 in (23 cm) in diameter and glue to center of circles as shown (e). This is paint can lid.

3. Before attaching the large circle lid to the hat cylinder, cut one end of the hat cylinder at an angle, as shown (f).

4. Glue the large circle to the slanted end of the cylinder (g).

5. Cover the top of the hat with glue and cover with aluminum foil.

6. Paint the underside of the circle and the sides of the cylinder the color of the paint in the can (Sea Blue).

7. Drip more of this color on the large body cylinder from the top edge and down over the sides of the "can" (h).

8. You may also paint the child's face with face paint to match the paint color.

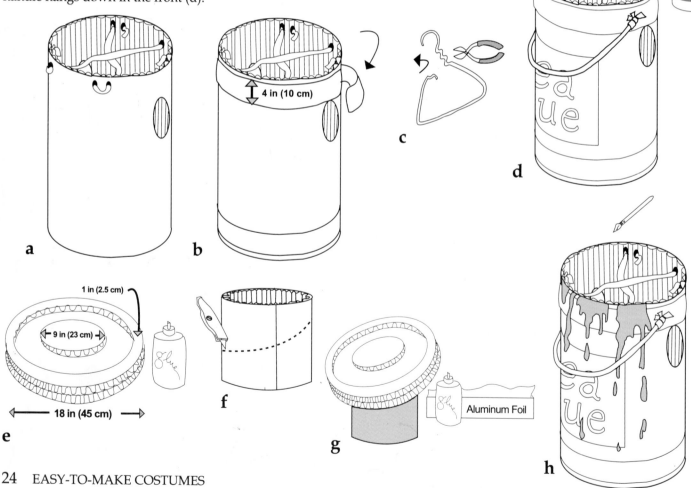

a

b

4 in (10 cm)

c

d

1 in (2.5 cm)

9 in (23 cm)

18 in (45 cm)

e

f

g

Aluminum Foil

h

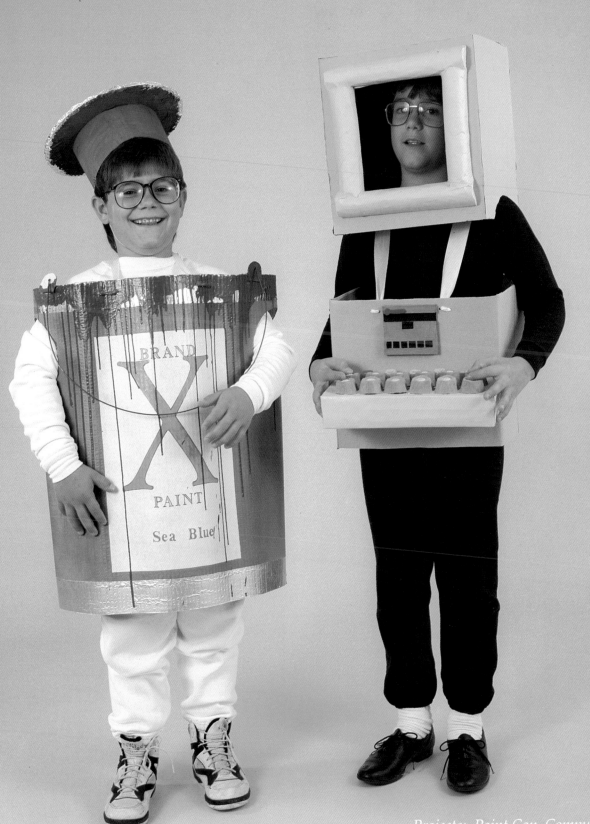

Computer

C

1. **Make Basic Box C** p 11. Wrap the box with grey or tan paper. Glue the paper to outside of box (a).

2. For the keyboard, wrap a long flat box with grey or tan paper and glue on. Cut out the cups from an egg carton and glue in rows on the top of the keyboard box, as shown (b). Paint grey.

3. Glue the side of the keyboard box to the front of the large box, as shown (c).

4. Cut out a piece of cardboard about 6 in (15 cm) square. With a sharp knife, cut out slots in the square to resemble the disk panel on a computer, as shown (d). Paint grey.

5. Glue to the front of the body box (e).

To Make Computer Screen Hat

1. Select a box that fits over the child's head comfortably. Cut out the bottom of the box. Cut out half circles from the bottom of each side, as shown (f), so that the box will sit on the child's shoulders. Cut out a square hole in the center of the front for the face.

2. Cover the box with grey or tan paper. Attach with glue.

3. For the screen frame, you will need 2 cardboard cylinders such as those from paper towels. Cut these in half along the length (g). Measure the size of the face hole, and cut these to length so that they will frame the face hole, as shown.

5. Cover cylinders with grey or tan paper. Glue on (h).

6. Glue pieces around the face hole, as shown (i).

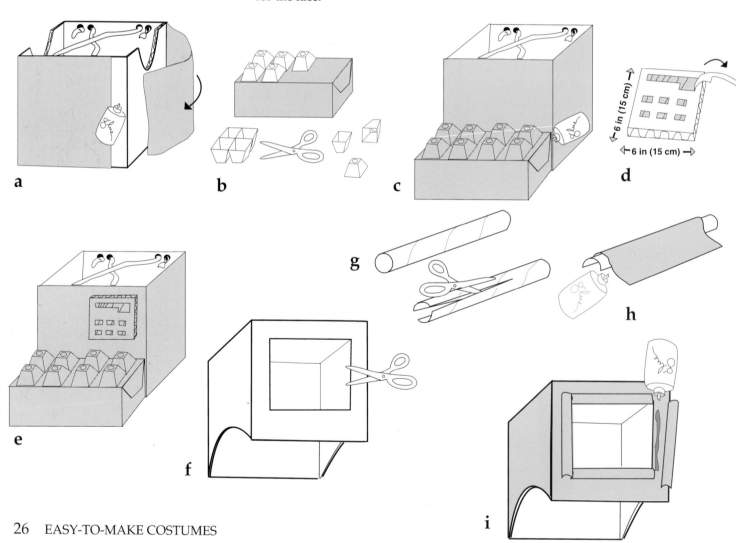

a

b

c

d

e

f

g

h

i

D&E&H

Princess

Materials

2 lengths plus sleeve length soft opaque fabric

3/4 yd (.7 m) white fake fur fabric

3/4 yd (.7 m) glitter fabric for bolero

2 yds (2 m) gold braid 1/2 in (1 cm) wide

3/4 yd (.7 m) gold lamé or gold foil

1/2 yd (.5 m) chiffon or a sheer scarf

To Make Dress

1. **Make Basic Tunic D** p 12, but use full sleeve, p 13. Adjust length to fit child. Turn up hem and stitch. Hem sleeves.

2. Mark waist of child. Sew 1-in (2.5-cm)-wide tape on wrong side for elastic casing (a). Thread through elastic. Adjust to waist measurement. Cut off excess. Sew ends.

3. Cut a strip of fake fur 3 in (7.5 cm) wide and tack to bottom of skirt hem. Cut 5 more strips, each 2 in (5 cm) wide and tack around sleeves and neck, as shown (b).

To Make Bolero

1. **Make Basic Vest E** p 14. Cut off for lace vest as marked. Hem all edges.

2. Sew gold braid around all outside edges of bolero (c).

To Make Hat

1. **Make Basic Cone Hat H** p 15.

2. Drape gold lamé or foil around outside of cone and allow material to overlap 3/4 in (2 cm) along seam. Cut off excess. Turn under at bottom, as shown (d).

3. Put glue all over outside of cone hat and inside edge and glue lamé or foil to cone. Allow to dry.

4. Glue wide gold braid around hat, as shown (e).

5. Glue sheer material by one point to point of cone and allow end to hang down (f).

6. Cut 2 pieces of gold lamé (or other soft material) each 4 in (10 cm) wide and 24 in (61 cm) long. Turn under sides and one end. Stitch. Glue unhemmed end to inside of each side of hat, as shown (g). These are the ties. Cross under chin and tie at back.

7. The child may wear gold necklace and gold chain around waist.

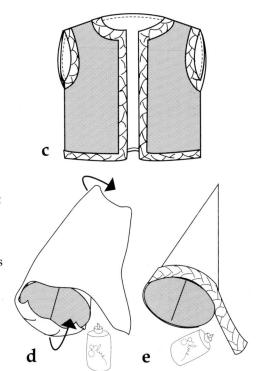

c

d

e

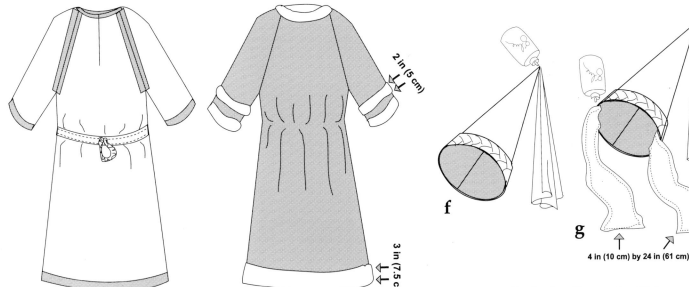

a

b

2 in (5 cm)

3 in (7.5 cm)

f

g

4 in (10 cm) by 24 in (61 cm)

D&E&G

King

Materials

2 lengths plus sleeve length velvet, velveteen, or any other rich looking fabric

1 yd (1 m) fake fur

3 yds (3 m) gold braid

To Make Robe

1. **Make Basic Tunic D** p 12, but use full sleeve, p 13.

2. Sew 2 rows of gold braid around sleeves and around tunic bottom, as shown (a).

3. Cut 4— 6 in (15 cm) pieces of gold braid. Fold each in half and tack one folded end to each sleeve and 2 folded ends to front hem of robe (a).

4. Wear loose gold chain or belt around robe. This will hold the sword as well.

To Make Fur Cloak

1. **Make Basic Vest E** p 14 as indicated for cloak, making rounded front. Lengthen pattern to fit the child's height. Fur cloak may be as long as you wish. A full length cloak will require more material.

2. Fake fur cut edges do not need to be hemmed or bound.

To Make Crown

1. **Make Basic Cylinder Hat G** p 15. Before rolling the strip of cardboard into a circle, cut the top edge into a fancy shape, as shown (c). Fasten in a circle (d).

2. Cover with metallic paper and decorate, as desired.

To Make Sword

1. Place 3 double sheets of newspaper one on top of the other. Roll from the long side, as shown (e). Glue loose edges and tape.

2. Flatten the roll. Fold the corners of one end to make a point. Glue and tape (f).

3. Roll up a single sheet of newspaper from the short end. Glue the loose edge.

4. Flatten the ends and roll each up 2 in (5 cm), as shown (g). Tape.

5. Turn on its side and flatten the middle of this roll. This is the handle guard.

6. Place the handle guard 12 in (30 cm) from the end of the larger tube and tape in place (h).

7. Fold up the end of the larger tube so that it lies over the guard, as shown. Glue and tape. This forms the handle. When the glue is dry, remove the tape (i).

8. Cover with metallic paper and decorate, as desired.

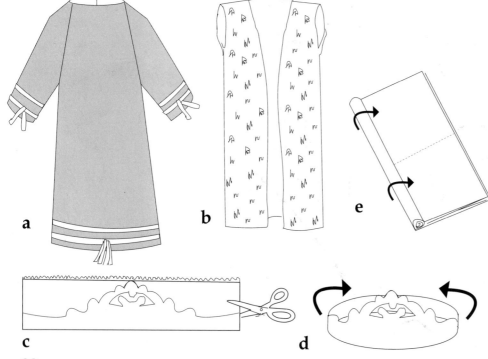

a

b

e

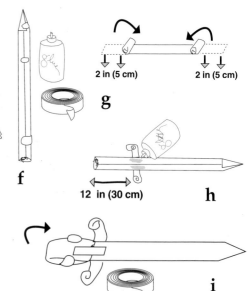

f

g

2 in (5 cm)   2 in (5 cm)

12 in (30 cm)   h

c

d

i

Computer

C

1. **Make Basic Box C** p 11. Wrap the box with grey or tan paper. Glue the paper to outside of box (a).

2. For the keyboard, wrap a long flat box with grey or tan paper and glue on. Cut out the cups from an egg carton and glue in rows on the top of the keyboard box, as shown (b). Paint grey.

3. Glue the side of the keyboard box to the front of the large box, as shown (c).

4. Cut out a piece of cardboard about 6 in (15 cm) square. With a sharp knife, cut out slots in the square to resemble the disk panel on a computer, as shown (d). Paint grey.

5. Glue to the front of the body box (e).

To Make Computer Screen Hat

1. Select a box that fits over the child's head comfortably. Cut out the bottom of the box. Cut out half circles from the bottom of each side, as shown (f), so that the box will sit on the child's shoulders. Cut out a square hole in the center of the front for the face.

2. Cover the box with grey or tan paper. Attach with glue.

3. For the screen frame, you will need 2 cardboard cylinders such as those from paper towels. Cut these in half along the length (g). Measure the size of the face hole, and cut these to length so that they will frame the face hole, as shown.

5. Cover cylinders with grey or tan paper. Glue on (h).

6. Glue pieces around the face hole, as shown (i).

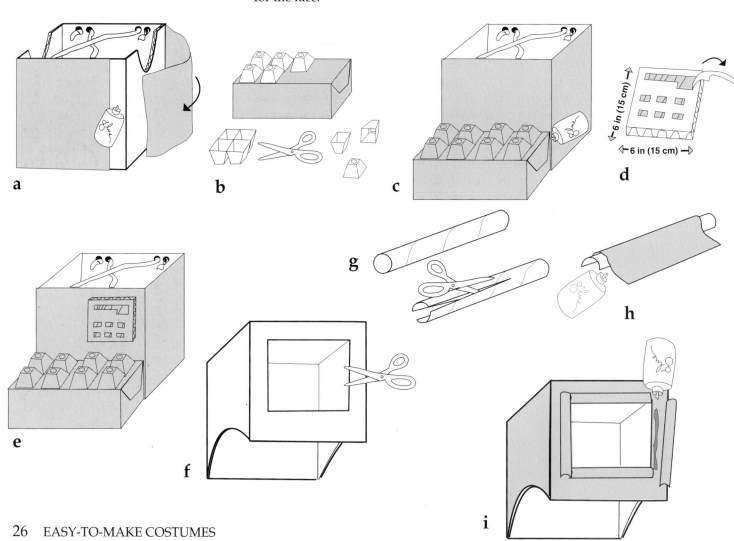

a

b

c

d 6 in (15 cm) 6 in (15 cm)

e

f

g

h

i

D&E&H

Princess

Materials

2 lengths plus sleeve length soft
  opaque fabric

3/4 yd (.7 m) white fake fur fabric

3/4 yd (.7 m) glitter fabric for bolero

2 yds (2 m) gold braid 1/2 in (1 cm)
  wide

3/4 yd (.7 m) gold lamé or gold foil

1/2 yd (.5 m) chiffon or a sheer scarf

To Make Dress

1. **Make Basic Tunic D** p 12, but use
full sleeve, p 13. Adjust length to fit
child. Turn up hem and stitch. Hem
sleeves.

2. Mark waist of child. Sew 1-in (2.5-
cm)-wide tape on wrong side for
elastic casing (a). Thread through
elastic. Adjust to waist measurement.
Cut off excess. Sew ends.

3. Cut a strip of fake fur 3 in (7.5 cm)
wide and tack to bottom of skirt hem.
Cut 5 more strips, each 2 in (5 cm)
wide and tack around sleeves and
neck, as shown (b).

To Make Bolero

1. **Make Basic Vest E** p 14. Cut off for
lace vest as marked. Hem all edges.

2. Sew gold braid around all outside
edges of bolero (c).

To Make Hat

1. **Make Basic Cone Hat H** p 15.

2. Drape gold lamé or foil around
outside of cone and allow material to
overlap 3/4 in (2 cm) along seam.
Cut off excess. Turn under at bottom,
as shown (d).

3. Put glue all over outside of cone hat
and inside edge and glue lamé or foil
to cone. Allow to dry.

4. Glue wide gold braid around hat, as
shown (e).

5. Glue sheer material by one point to
point of cone and allow end to hang
down (f).

6. Cut 2 pieces of gold lamé (or other

soft material) each 4 in (10 cm) wide
and 24 in (61 cm) long. Turn under
sides and one end. Stitch. Glue
unhemmed end to inside of each side
of hat, as shown (g). These are the
ties. Cross under chin and tie at back.

7. The child may wear gold necklace
and gold chain around waist.

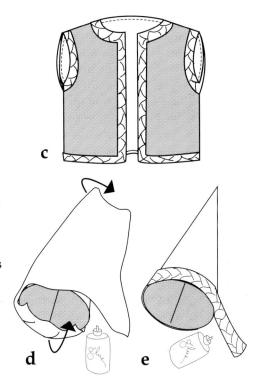

c

a

b

2 in (5 cm)

3 in (7.5 cm)

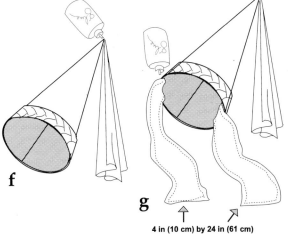

d

e

f

g

4 in (10 cm) by 24 in (61 cm)

Projects: Computer, Princess 27

D&E&G

King

Materials

2 lengths plus sleeve length velvet, velveteen, or any other rich looking fabric

1 yd (1 m) fake fur

3 yds (3 m) gold braid

To Make Robe

1. **Make Basic Tunic D** p 12, but use full sleeve, p 13.

2. Sew 2 rows of gold braid around sleeves and around tunic bottom, as shown (a).

3. Cut 4— 6 in (15 cm) pieces of gold braid. Fold each in half and tack one folded end to each sleeve and 2 folded ends to front hem of robe (a).

4. Wear loose gold chain or belt around robe. This will hold the sword as well.

To Make Fur Cloak

1. **Make Basic Vest E** p 14 as indicated for cloak, making rounded front. Lengthen pattern to fit the child's height. Fur cloak may be as long as you wish. A full length cloak will require more material.

2. Fake fur cut edges do not need to be hemmed or bound.

To Make Crown

1. **Make Basic Cylinder Hat G** p 15. Before rolling the strip of cardboard into a circle, cut the top edge into a fancy shape, as shown (c). Fasten in a circle (d).

2. Cover with metallic paper and decorate, as desired.

To Make Sword

1. Place 3 double sheets of newspaper one on top of the other. Roll from the long side, as shown (e). Glue loose edges and tape.

2. Flatten the roll. Fold the corners of one end to make a point. Glue and tape (f).

3. Roll up a single sheet of newspaper from the short end. Glue the loose edge.

4. Flatten the ends and roll each up 2 in (5 cm), as shown (g). Tape.

5. Turn on its side and flatten the middle of this roll. This is the handle guard.

6. Place the handle guard 12 in (30 cm) from the end of the larger tube and tape in place (h).

7. Fold up the end of the larger tube so that it lies over the guard, as shown. Glue and tape. This forms the handle. When the glue is dry, remove the tape (i).

8. Cover with metallic paper and decorate, as desired.

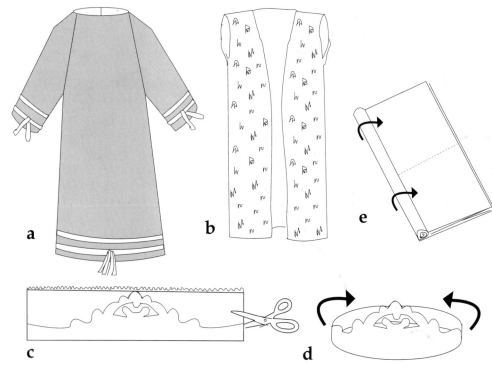

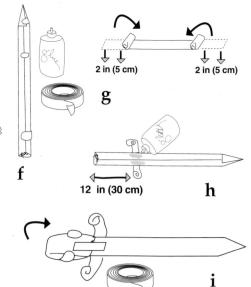

Laundry Hamper

1. **Make Basic Box C** p 11. When cutting off flaps, **leave one flap on the back side of the box at the top** for the hamper lid, as shown (a).

2. Cover the box with wallpaper or shelf paper that has a wood grain or wicker pattern. If paper is not self-adhesive, attach with glue (b).

3. Make a handle for each side of the box by cutting out a rectangle 3 in (8 cm) long and 1 in (2.5 cm) wide on each side of the box (c). Draw a line around the cut-out rectangles, 1/2 in (1 cm) outside the cut lines on three sides, as shown (d). Cut out along this drawn line (e). Fold upwards, as shown (f).

4. Cut out a small hook shape from excess cardboard and attach it to the front of the box, as shown (g).

5. Tape old clothes around the top of the box, suggesting they are spilling out of the clothes hamper (h).

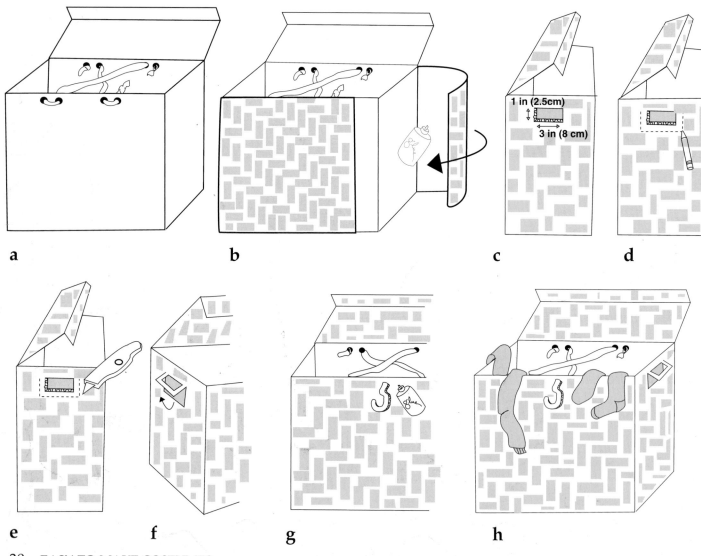

a

b

c

d

e

f

g

h

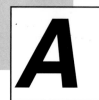

Bar of Soap

1. **Make Basic Cylinder A** p 8. Be sure the smooth side of the cardboard faces outward.

2. Glue strips of cardboard on the sides (on the inside) to hold the shape of the bar of soap, as shown (a).

3. Cut out a large rectangle from the front of the cylinder (b). Cut off 1/2 in (1 cm) from each side of the rectangle that has been removed (c).

4. Draw the letters for "SOAPY" on the rectangle. Draw them 1/2 in (1 cm) thick (d).

5. With a sharp knife, cut out the letters. Save the centers of the "O", "A", and the "P".

6. From another piece of smooth cardboard, cut out a rectangle that is slightly larger than the hole in the front of the cylinder, and glue this rectangle to the inside of the cylinder, covering the hole (e).

7. Glue the rectangle that says "SOAPY" to the center of the rectangle in the front of the cylinder. There should be a 1/2 in (1 cm) space all around the top rectangle. Glue the centers of the "O", "A", and the "P" in place (f).

8. Paint the cylinder white. Blow up clear balloons and tape or tie them on the cylinder to resemble soap bubbles.

d

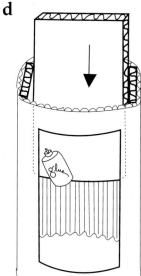

e

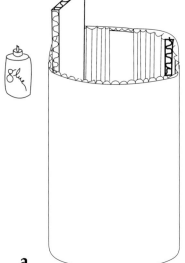

a

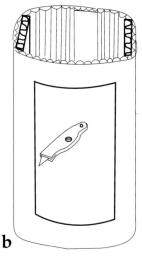

b

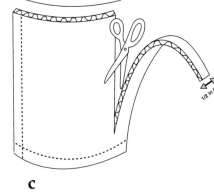

c

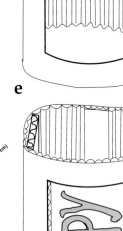

f

Ballerina

Materials
1 yd (1 m) red stiff tulle
elastic
red folded bias tape 1 in (2.5 cm)
  wide
2 yds (2 m) red ribbon 1 in (2.5 cm)
  wide
1/2 yd (.5 m) black lace remnant
black folded bias tape 1/2 in (1 cm)
  wide

Costume is assembled over red leotards, red turtleneck, and red ballet slippers.

To Make Tutu

1. Tulle is usually folded in 2 or 3 layers when purchased. Cut along the fold line at one side only to separate the layers (a).

2. Fold material short end to short end and stitch (b). Shorten skirt if needed.

3. Baste red folded tape over top edge of tutu and stitch leaving small opening. This is the elastic casing (c).

4. Thread elastic through casing. Adjust elastic to child's waist measurement. Cut off excess. Sew elastic ends together. Sew opening closed (d).

To Make Headband

1. Cover a hairband with red ribbon. Wrap ribbon snuggly around the hairband and tack in place (e).

2. Decorate the hairband with red bows, flower, or feathers (f).

To Make Bolero

1. **Make Basic Vest E** p 14 from black lace remnant. Try on and adjust length.

2. Bind all unhemmed edges with black bias tape (g).

3. Sew fasteners on front to close vest.

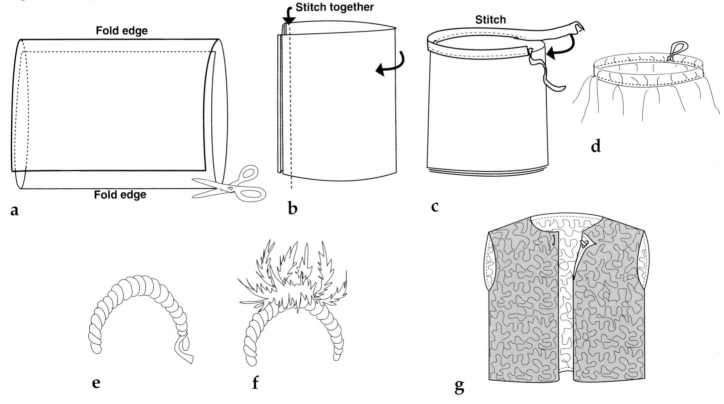

a   b   c   d

e   f   g

Projects: Bar of Soap, Ballerina   33

Elephant

Materials
1-1/2 yds (1.5 m) brightly colored soft
fabric
newspaper
paint
red ribbon for bow tie
Costume is assembled over plain grey
track suit.

To Make Skirt and Bow

1. Cut one piece of fabric 1-1/2 yds
(1.5 m) long and 14 in (35 cm) wide.
Cut another piece 1-1/2 yds (1.5 m)
long and 8 in (20 cm) wide. Pin one
piece over the other, right sides out, so
top ends are even (a).

2. Turn over waist hem allowance
and stitch on wrong side to make a
casing leaving a small opening to
insert elastic (b). Sew side seam on
each skirt layer.

3. Thread elastic through casing.
Measure waist size you need and cut
off excess. Sew elastic ends together.
Sew opening closed.

4. Turn up hem on each skirt layer
and stitch (c).

5. Make a large bow (d) from colored
ribbon or use an old scarf and attach
to front of track suit top.

To Make a Papier-mâché Face Mask

1. Glue 6 sheets of newspaper one on
top of the other.

2. Draw an elephant head shape
(large enough to cover child's face) on
the top sheet and cut out. Allow to
dry (e) .

3. Cut out holes for the eyes and
mouth (e).

4. Paint features for an elephant head,
as shown (e).

5. Make a trunk by rolling a double
sheet of newspaper diagonally into a
loose tube (f). Glue and tape. Place
tube on a broom handle. Grasp the
handle below the tube with one hand
and with the other hand slowly crush
the entire tube, as shown (g).

6. Glue the crushed tube to the face of
the elephant head and paint (h).

7. Glue string to sides of mask with
5-minute epoxy on back sides of mask,
as shown (h).

To Make Feet

1. Make 4 elephant feet using the
technique for the Reindeer p 57. Make
from smooth cardboard (i). Paint
grey with pink toenails.

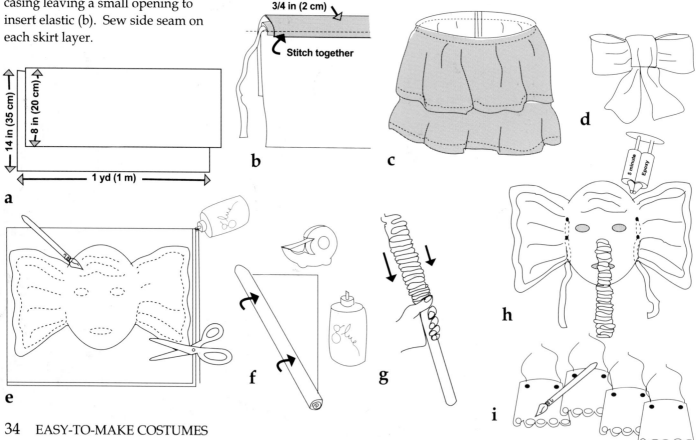

B

Cookie

1. **Make Basic Sandwich Board B** p 10 using 2 large circles for the front and back pieces, each 30 in (76 cm) in diameter (a).

2. Cover one large sheet of newspaper with glue and lay this on the front circle. Push the newspaper gently with your hands to form ridges and wrinkles to resemble the rough surface of a cookie (b).

3. Cut out the cardboard cups from an egg carton (c), and glue these randomly on the surface of the front section to resemble giant chocolate chips. Cover the edges of the cups with small pieces of newspaper and glue for a more finished look (d).

4. Paint the cardboard yellow-brown and the egg cups dark brown.

5. Paint the back board with more yellow-brown paint and brush a slightly darker brown lightly over the surface for a "baked" appearance.

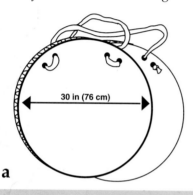

a

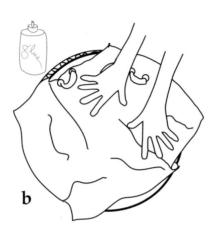

b

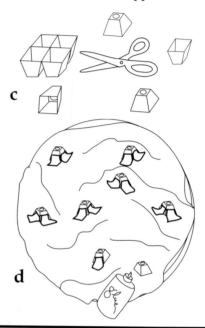

c

d

A

Vase of Flowers

1. **Make Basic Cylinder A** p 8. Make sure the smooth side of the cardboard faces outward.

2. Before gluing the ends of the cylinder together, cut the ends at a slight angle, as shown (a). Bring the 2 ends together, overlap, and glue so that cylinder is wider at the top than at the bottom (b).

3. Cut out armholes and add shoulder straps. Paint cylinder white.

4. Cut out pictures of flowers from magazines, or draw and color pictures of flowers and cut out. Arrange these on the front of the vase and glue in place (c). Decorate the cylinder edges with metallic paper, if desired.

5. Purchase artificial flowers with wire stems. With a sharp instrument make holes around rim of "vase." Insert the wire stems into the corrugated holes around the top of the vase, as shown (d), and secure.

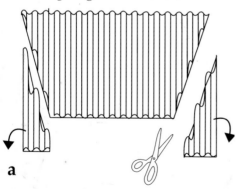

a

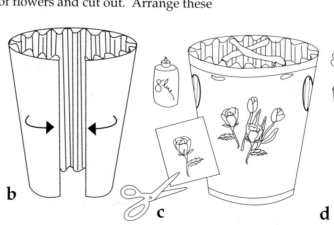

b

c

d

D

Bunny

Materials
2 lengths plus sleeve length of white fake fur
6 in (15 cm) pink felt, velvet, cotton, or satin for ears
buckram interfacing for ears
velcro for closures
white 3/4 in (2 cm) bias tape
white elastic

1. **Make Basic Tunic D with Legs** p 12. Fur does not fray so edges are not hemmed.

To Make Ears and Hood

1. Cut 4 bunny ears (b) from white fur fabric and 2 buckram interfacings the same size. Tack interfacing to wrong side of 2 ears, as shown (c).

2. Cut 2 pink liners, as indicated (b). If pink fabric frays, blind stitch around edges or turn edges under 1/4 in (.6 cm) and stitch.

3. Sew 1 pink liner to right side of ear that has interfacing (d). Pin ear to another bunny ear, right sides together (e). Stitch, leaving bottom open. Turn to right side. Repeat for second ear.

4. Cut out 2 hood pieces from white fur (b). Sew dart B on wrong sides. On right side of hood fold dart A dotted line to solid line and insert 1 ear (f) so pink liner faces front. Stitch on wrong side. Repeat for second piece.

5. Place right sides of hood pieces together and stitch leaving face and neck openings open, and leaving ears free (g). Turn to right side.

6. Sew velcro closing on neck flaps (h) to close under chin.

To Make Mitts

1. Cut 4 mitts (b). Pin right sides of 2 mitts together and stitch, leaving top open (i). Turn to right side. Repeat for second mitt.

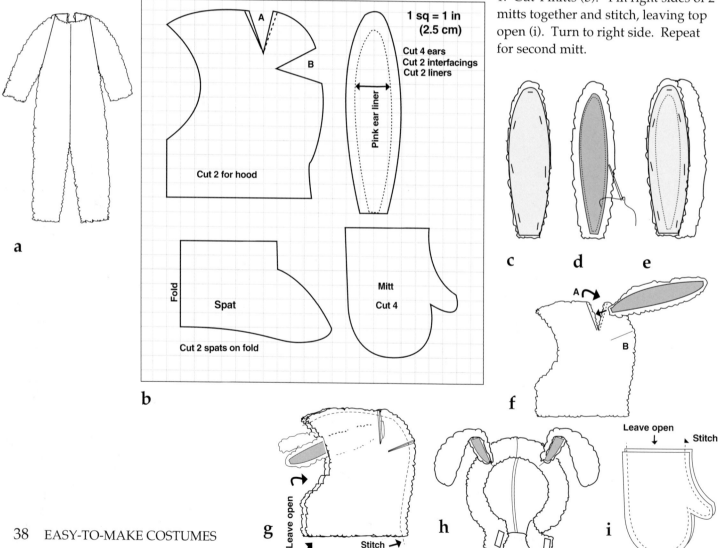

a

b

1 sq = 1 in (2.5 cm)

A
B

Cut 2 for hood

Pink ear liner

Cut 4 ears
Cut 2 interfacings
Cut 2 liners

Fold

Spat
Cut 2 spats on fold

Mitt
Cut 4

c   d   e

f

A

B

Leave open
Stitch

g
Leave open
Stitch

h

i
Leave open
Stitch

Bunny Costume continued.

To Make Spats

1. Place spats pattern on fold of material as indicated (b) and cut 2.

2. Lay spat out flat. Stitch white bias tape for elastic casing, as shown (j).

3. Pin right sides of each spat together and stitch, leaving top and bottom open, as well as casing opening for elastic (k).

4. Thread elastic through casing. Adjust ankle measurement. Sew ends of elastic together, as shown (k). Turn to right side. Repeat for second spat.

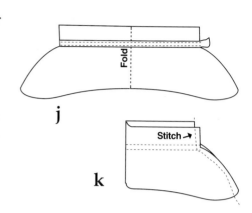

j

k

Use basic techniques

C&H

Jack-in-the-Box

1. **Make Basic Box C** p 11. NOTE: Cut off only 3 flaps at top end of box (a).

2. Cover box with wrapping paper of your choice (b). Glue on. Fold over edges and glue.

To Make Handle

1. Roll a piece of newspaper into a tight tube. Glue and cut, as shown (c).

2. Lay the tube vertically. Bend the top end down to the right, 3 in (7.5 cm) from the end. Bend the bottom end up to the left, 3 in (7.5 cm) from the bottom, as shown (d).

3. Cut 2 strips of newspaper 1 in (2.5 cm) wide and 8 in (20 cm) long (e). Spread glue over one side of each strip and wrap one strip around each bend to hold it in place. Tape if necessary until dry.

4. Glue one end to the side of the box

(f). Paint or cover with metallic paper.

To Make Hat

1. **Make Basic Cone Hat H** p 15.

2. Cover the cone with the same wrapping paper used to cover the box (g). Fold over edges and glue.

3. Make a pom-pom for the top. Lay 2 pieces of tissue paper or facial tissue one on top of the other. Pleat them together starting at the short end (h). Tie in the middle with string, as shown (i). Carefully separate the layers to make a fluffy ball.

5. Glue the pom-pom to the top of the cone (j).

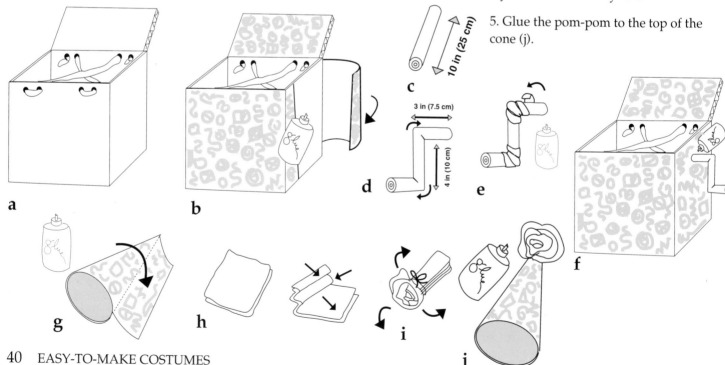

a

b

c

10 in (25 cm)

3 in (7.5 cm)

4 in (10 cm)

d

e

f

g

h

i

j

Pea Pod

A&F

1. **Make Basic Cylinder A** p 8. Be sure the smooth side of the cardboard faces outward (a). Do not make arm allowance.

2. Cut 2 pieces of cardboard, 1 yd (1 m) long and 2 ft (60 cm) wide. Lay the 2 pieces one on top of the other, rippled sides together, and glue them together along one long side. Staple together for strength, as shown (b).

3. When dry, set upright at the back of the cylinder and wrap each piece around the cylinder, as shown (c). Glue and staple in place, leaving 12 in (30 cm) at the front of the cylinder uncovered.

4. With sharp scissors, cut the outside layer of cardboard in a smooth curve, starting at the back of the costume at the top and cutting downward to the front to be as high as the basic cylinder, as shown (d).

5. Paint the entire costume bright green. Allow the outside layer to curl back naturally (it will do this when it is wet with paint and drying) (e).

6. When dry, punch pairs of holes in a row down the front of the costume. Leave 4 in (10 cm) between the pairs, as shown (e).

7. Blow up as many round green balloons as there are pairs of holes, and knot each balloon. Cut pieces of string 8 in (20 cm) long and tie to the balloons so that there are 2 equal pieces of string hanging, approx. 4 in (10 cm) long. Thread the string through the holes and tie on the inside of the costume, as shown (f). The balloons are the peas.

8. Bend one green pipe cleaner into a gentle curve, and glue this to the front of the outer layer of cardboard (g). This is the tendril.

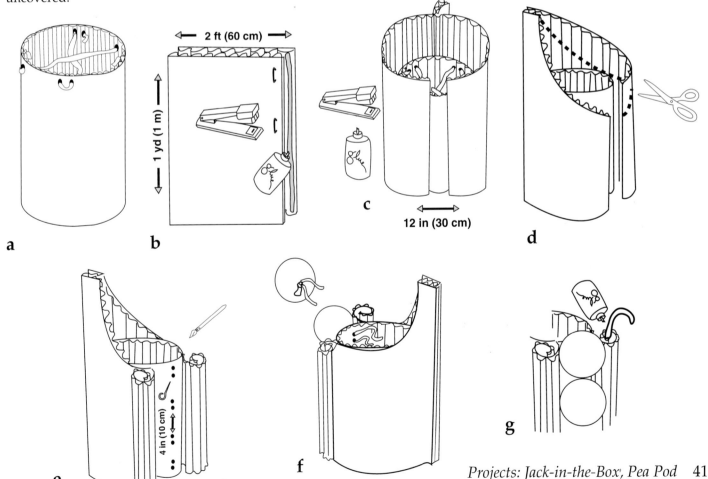

a

b — 2 ft (60 cm) — 1 yd (1 m)

c — 12 in (30 cm)

d

e — 4 in (10 cm)

f

g

Projects: Jack-in-the-Box, Pea Pod 41

Pea Pod Costume continued.
To Make Hat

1. **Make Basic Bowl Hat F** p 14 (no brim).

2. Cut out 6 leaves 4 in (10 cm) long and 2 in (5 cm) wide from green construction paper, or white paper painted green (h). Paint the hat green. Glue the leaves to top of the hat (i).

3. Curl 2 green pipe cleaners around your finger to make a corkscrew shape (j). Glue these to the top of the hat (k). These are the tendrils.

4. Paint the child's face green with face paint if you wish.

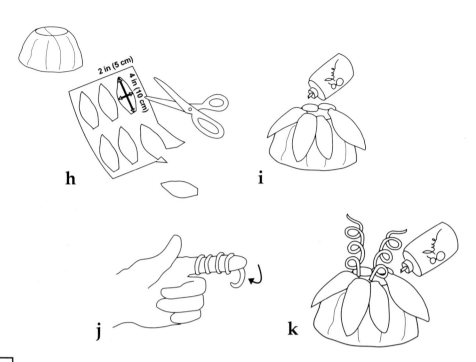

Use basic technique

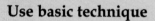

Soup Can

1. **Make Basic Cylinder A** p 8 with armholes. Be sure the smooth side of the cardboard faces outward (a).

2. Cut a large circle, 18 in (45 cm) in diameter, from smooth, firm cardboard (b). This will be the lid of the opened can.

3. Spread glue over one side of the circle and cover with aluminum foil. Cover the other side with foil in the same way, but leave 2 in (5 cm) on one side of the circle uncovered, as shown (c).

4. Glue this uncovered edge to the inside edge of the back of the cylinder, as shown (d). Fold back slightly. Allow to dry.

5. Paint the cylinder to resemble a soup can with a label on the front (e).

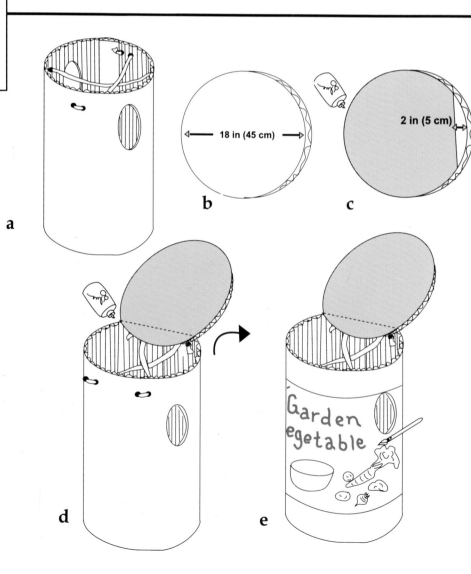

Skeleton

This costume is worn over a black track suit.

1. Lay the track suit flat. Refer to grid (a) and transfer bone shapes to paper pattern (a). Cut out pattern pieces. Lay paper patterns on firm, smooth cardboard and trace outlines. Cut out.

2. Paint the bones white and shellac. Allow to dry.

3. Punch a single hole in the ends of the bones where they will connect (b). Hook the bones together with paper clips, as shown (c).

4. Glue pieces of black ribbon to the back of the skeleton with 5-minute epoxy at the waist, neck, wrists, and ankles, as shown (d). Cut the ribbons long enough to tie around the child. This will hold the skeleton in place.

5. **To make skeleton feet**, place child's feet on firm, smooth cardboard and trace around front parts of child's feet (exclude heels). Cut out (e). Punch 1 hole at each side, as shown (f). Thread with string and tie around child's ankles (g).

6. Draw foot bones on top. Paint black with white bones.

7. Paint the child's face to resemble a skull.

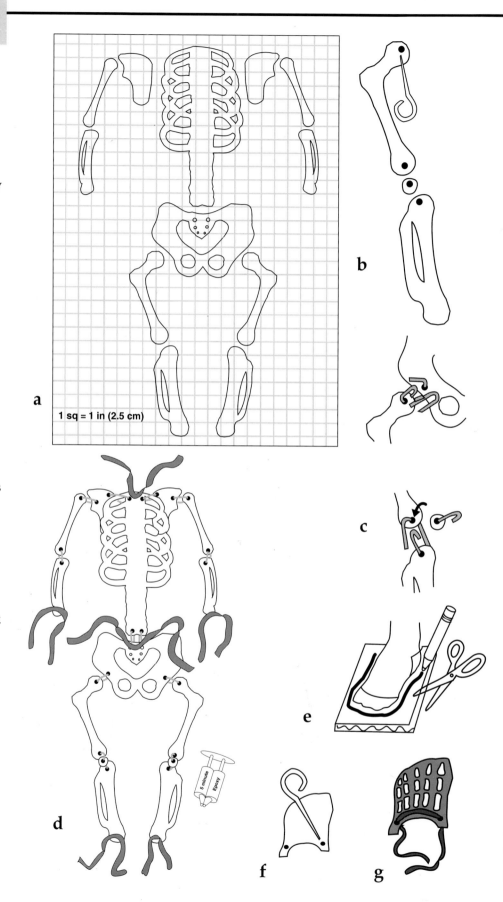

1 sq = 1 in (2.5 cm)

D&F

Pirate

Materials

2 lengths plus sleeve length red
velvet, velveteen, or other rich
looking fabric for jacket
2 lengths plus sleeve length white
satin or other shiny white fabric for
blouse
1 yd (1 m) white folded bias binding
1 in (2.5 cm) wide
white cotton scraps for interfacing
3 yds (3 m) gold braid
1/4 yd (.25 m) gold fabric for cuffs
1 yd (1 m) white lace, 5 in (12.5 cm)
wide

To Make Jacket

1. **Make Basic Tunic D** p 12. Place
back on fold, cut 2 fronts. Cut off for
jacket, round neck fronts (a). Stitch
hem on neck, fronts, and bottom.

To Make Cuffs

1. Measure around bottom of sleeve.
Make cuffs 2 in (5 cm) longer and 4 in
(10 cm) wide (b). Cut 4.

2. Cut 2 interfacing pieces same size
from scraps of cotton. Place 2 right
sides of cuffs together with 1 interfacing piece on outside of top cuff.
Stitch along sides and top (c).

3. Turn cuffs to right side. Press.

4. Pin unstitched side to right side of
sleeve, as shown (d). Stitch. Turn up
(e). Repeat for other cuff.

5. Tack gold braid around top of cuffs
and down fronts of jacket (f).

To Make Blouse

1. **Make Basic Tunic D** p 12 but cut
off at where marked for blouse. Do
not hem neck or sew side sleeve
seams yet (g).

2. **Make separate dickie.** Cut 2 pieces
of wide lace each 6 in (15 cm) long.
Stitch one over the other, as shown
(h). Gather neck edge and baste to
right side of neck front. Bind
complete neck edge and neck opening
with white folded bias binding (i).
Sew on velcro for back neck closing.

3. Cut 2 pieces of lace same size as
sleeve bottom. Stitch l to each sleeve
(j) right sides together. Allow lace to
hang down.

4. Sew unfolded 1-in (2.5-cm) -wide
white bias tape to inside of sleeve (k).
This is elastic casing.

5. Sew sleeve, lace cuff, and side
seams of tunic together and hem
bottom. Thread elastic through casing.
Sew ends closed (l).

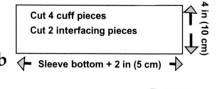

Pirate Costume continued.

6. Complete the costume with a purchased wide black belt, black track suit trousers, high black rain boots, and eye patch.

To Make Hat

1. **Make Basic Bowl Hat F** p 14. Leave a wide newpaper brim around bowl hat.

2. While wet, fold brim up against the crown on one side (m). Allow to dry.

3. Paint hat black.

4. On a piece of white paper draw a skull and crossbones. Use a black felt marker (n). Paint black around skull and cross bones to match hat. Cut out square. Glue to front of hat.

To Make Pirate Hook

1. Straighten a wire coat hanger, leaving the hook intact (o).

2. Cut off the wire 8 in (20 cm) from the base of the hook (p).

3. Bend the straight wire into an oval loop that is easy to grip. Tape in place with strong tape such as duct tape.

4. Cover the hook with more duct tape making sure the end of the hook is blunted for safety (q).

5. Cut a strip of corrugated cardboard 4 in (10 cm) wide and 12 in (30 cm) long (measure length **across** ripples).

Fit the ends together so that the child can fit his hand inside it (r).

6. Cut off the excess and tape together. Put the ring on cardboard and trace around it (s). Cut out the circle.

7. Poke a hole in the center of the circle and push the hook through the hole, right through to the base of the hook (t). Tape the circle to the top of the cardboard ring so that the wire loop is inside the cardboard ring (u).

9. Cover with duct tape (u).

To Make Sword (v)

See instructions for King's sword p 28.

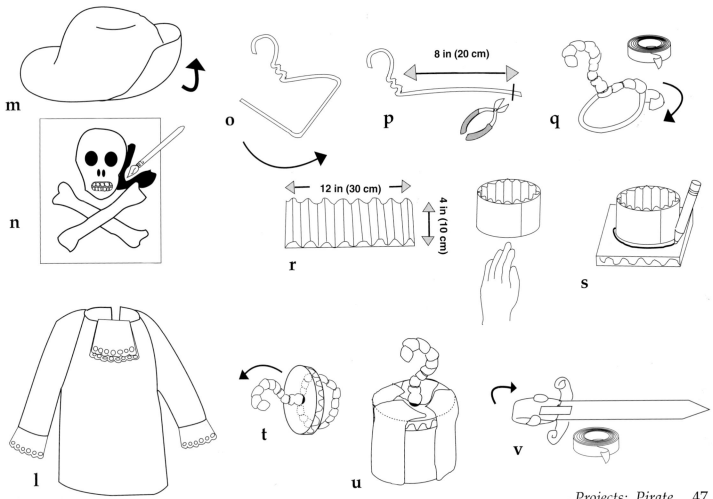

Projects: Nativity Scene 49

D

Mary

Materials
2 lengths plus length of sleeve of
 heavy white fabric that will drape
velcro
bias tape to secure gathered neck
2 yd (2 m) square of pale blue heavy
 fabric that will drape
3 yd (3 m) braided cotton rope

1. **Make Basic Tunic D** (Variation including full sleeve) p 12. Leave sleeves hanging loose. Hem edges (a). Use 2 yd (2 m) braided rope for belt.

To Make Veil

1. Place blue fabric on a firm surface.

2. Using a large dinner plate and a

a

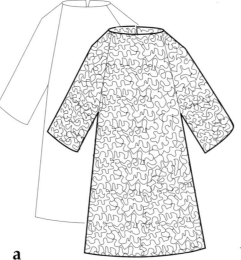

b

marker draw half circles along the edge of the fabric (b).

3. Cut along the curved edge to make a scalloped edge. Hem by hand or serge with an overlock machine.

4. Place veil over child's head. Secure with 1 yd (1 m) of braided rope for headband (c). Tie rope in knot at back.

Option: If you do not wish to have the scalloped edge effect, hem the square of blue fabric.

c

D

Angel

Materials
2 lengths plus length of sleeve of
 white cotton
2 lengths plus length of sleeve of
gold sheer fabric
5 yds (5 m) fine gold braid
gold crepe ribbon
lightweight wire

1. **Make 2 Basic Tunics D** (Variation including full sleeves) p 12, one of white cotton for the under gown and one of gold sheer fabric for the over gown (a). Sleeves hang loose. Hem edges.

2. Trim over gown with gold braid, if desired.

a

3. Soak several 1/2 yd (.5 m) pieces of fine gold braid with hair spray (b). Wind around several curlers and spray again with hairspray. Unwind only when ready to wear costume. Attach these "curls" to hair for shimmering look.

4. Wear purchased gold tinsel tiara.

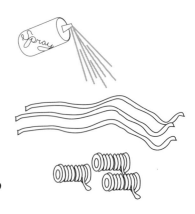

b

Angel Costume continued.

To Make Angel Wings

1. Straighten 2 wire coat hangers. Cut off the hook (c).

2. Bend each wire into a wing shape, as shown (d). Fit the curled end to the child so that it fits comfortably over shoulder and under the armpit.

3. Wrap gold crepe ribbon around each wire (e). Tape in place.

4. With light wire, attach the 2 wing shapes together. Cross the 2 lighter wires in an "X" in the center and wrap around each other attaching the ends to the coat hangers, as shown (f).

5. Cut many 8 in (20 cm) lengths of gold crepe ribbon. Round the ends of the ribbon to resemble feather tips (g).

6. Tie the ribbon feathers to the coat hangers by knotting the ribbon in the center, leaving the 2 — 4 in (10 cm) ends sticking up. Cover the wings with these ribbon feathers (h).

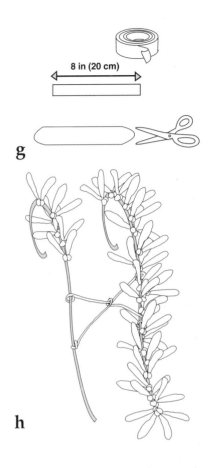

8 in (20 cm)

c   d   e   f   g   h

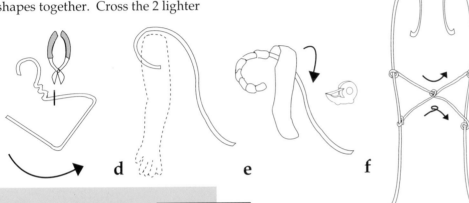

Use basic technique D

Three Wisemen

Materials
2 lengths plus sleeve length of 3 different colored fabrics: any soft fabric that looks rich and drapes well will do.

3 yds (3 m) fancy cord or rope for headbands

3 different colored pieces of fabric, each 1 yd (1 m) square for head pieces

1. **Make 3 Basic Tunics D** (Variation including full sleeves) p 12, each from different fabrics and choosing different colors. Mix and match costume if you wish, depending on fabric you have (a). Sleeves hang loose. Hem edges.

2. Make 3 belts from contrasting fabric. You will need a piece 2 yds (2 m) long and 6 in (15 cm) wide (b) for each belt.

3. Fold right sides together and stitch at seam allowance around 3 sides. Leave end open. Turn. Fold under

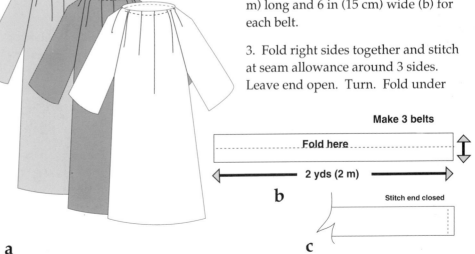

Make 3 belts

Fold here

2 yds (2 m)

b

Stitch end closed

c

a

Wisemen Costumes continued.
open end and stitch (c). Press. Tie
around waist.

To Make Head Pieces

1. Hem edges of three 1 yd (1 m)
square pieces of colored material (d).
Place one square over each child's
head. Hold in place with a rope or
cord headband, knotted at the back of
the head, as shown (e).

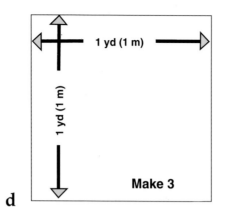

1 yd (1 m)

1 yd (1 m)

Make 3

d

e

No basic technique required.
Instructions complete on pp 52 and 53

Three Wisemen's Gifts

To Make Gift Box

1. Wrap small cardboard box with
metallic paper (a).

2. Cut out pieces of a different color
metallic paper, each slightly smaller
than one of the sides of the box (b).

3. Fold the paper several times.

4. Cut small pieces out of the edges of
the folded paper, as shown (c).

5. Unfold the paper and glue the cut-
out to the box (d). Additional
decoration may be added, as desired.

a

b

c

d

To Make Incense Holder

1. Cover a plastic bottle with metallic
paper, fitting it tightly to the neck (e).
Cover the top as well. Glue and tape.

2. Cut a piece of corrugated cardboard
across the ripples, 10 in (25 cm) long
and 2 in (5 cm) wide. Cut a half circle
out of each end (f).

3. Cover the cardboard strip with
fancy paper.

4. Tape the rounded ends to the neck
of the bottle so that it loops up and
over to form a handle (g). Cover the
join with a pipe cleaner or more
paper.

5. Additional decoration may be
added, as desired.

e

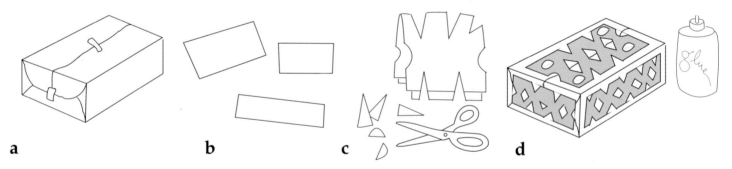

2 in (5 cm)

f

10 in (25 cm)

g

Wisemen's Gifts continued.

To Make Treasure Chest

1. Choose a square cardboard box with a lid.

2. Cut a piece of corrugated cardboard as wide as the lid and 3 in (7.5 cm) longer than the lid. Cut **across** the ripples so that the cardboard will arch from front to back (h).

3. Arch the cardboard and glue it to the top of the lid, making a curved lid. Hold the curve in place with tape, until the glue dries (i).

4. When dry, lay the box on its side and trace around the lid. Use a ruler to mark across the bottom of the arch, as shown (j). Cut out. Repeat on the other side. This makes 2 sides for the lid. Glue and tape the sides in place.

5. Cover the box with wood grain patterned paper.

6. Measure the front and back sides of the box. Cut 2 strips of cardboard for each side the same height as the box and 1-1/2 in (4 cm) wide (k).

7. Cover with metallic paper or aluminum foil. Attach 2 pieces to each side, as shown (l).

8. Measure the distance over the top of the box. Draw decorative ends on cardboard for 2 more strips 1-1/2 in (4 cm) wide and long enough to go over the lid. Cut out (m).

10. Cover strips with metallic paper or foil, and glue in place on the lid, as shown (n).

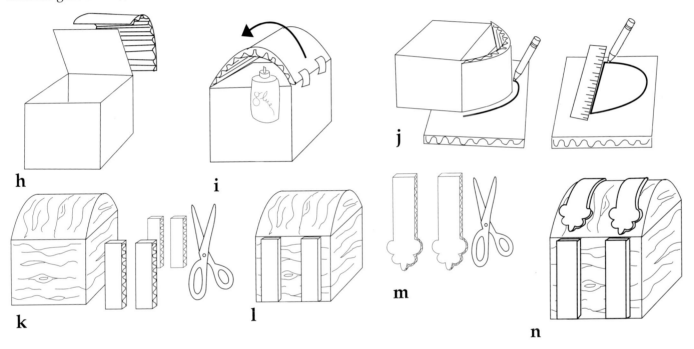

h

i

j

k

l

m

n

Manger

1. Cut off the top of a large cardboard box (a).

2. Cover the outside with wood or sticks (b). Bark is easily pulled off rotted logs found in the woods. Use plenty of wood glue, taking care to protect the working surface with newspaper. Cover one side at a time until the glue dries.

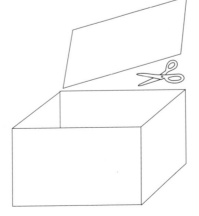

a

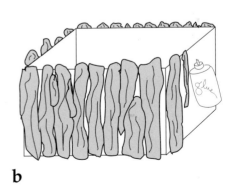

b

Valentine

B

1. Make Basic Sandwich Board B
p 10 using a heart shape, 30 in (72 cm) wide by 24 in (48 cm) long.

2. To make a lace border for the valentine you will need several sheets of letter size white paper. Cut each sheet in half so that the pieces are 4 in (10 cm) wide and 11 in (28 cm) long (b).

3. Fold the paper into a small rectangle. With sharp scissors, cut small pieces out of the folded edges (c). When you unfold the paper, there will be many holes throughout the paper, as shown (d). This is the lace.

4. Glue the pieces of paper around the back edges of the front heart shape (e).

5. Paint heart pink.

6. Cut out a number of small hearts from red paper and glue around the edge of the heart shape, as shown (f). Use purchased cupid or cut out a large cupid with bow and arrow from red paper and glue to center of heart shape (g).

8. The child can wear red leotards and turtleneck and a red hairband or bow to complete the outfit. Paint child's cheeks with hearts.

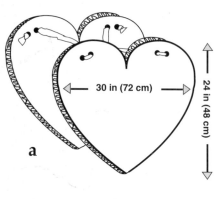

a

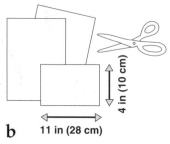

b

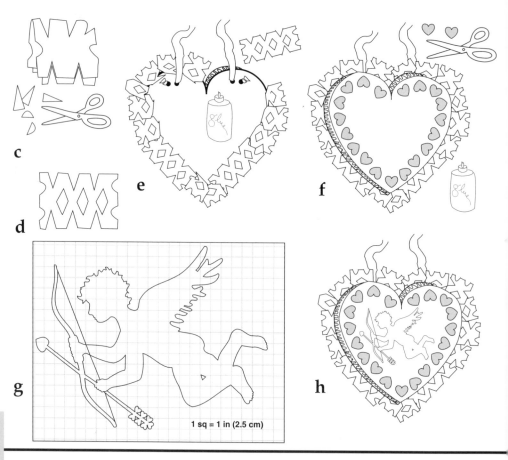

g   1 sq = 1 in (2.5 cm)

No basic technique required.
Instructions complete on pp 54 and 56

Bride

Materials
2-1/4 yds (2.3 m) white fabric
white bias tape (unfolded) 1 in (2.5 cm) wide
white elastic
white lace
headband
white tulle
artificial flowers

To Make Skirt

1. Select any white material (preferably opaque and crease resistant) that will drape well. Cut 2 lengths of fabric 1 yd (1 m) wide and skirt length required for your child.

2. Pin right sides of fabric together and stitch side seams (a). Press seams open. Turn to right side.

Bride Costume continued.

3. Sew tape to right side of fabric, as shown (b). Turn to inside and stitch, leaving small opening. This is the elastic casing.

4. Thread elastic through casing. Measure child's waist. Cut elastic. Sew ends together and sew opening closed (c). Try skirt on child. Adjust the gathers.

5. Measure the length and turn under and stitch hem. Press. Sew lace around bottom if you wish (d).

To Make Top

1. Cut 2 pieces of white fabric 12 in (30 cm) long and 20 in (51 cm) wide. Pin right sides together and stitch side seams (e). Press. Turn to right side.

2. Sew tape to right side along top edge. Turn to inside and stitch, leaving a small opening as in skirt (b). This is the elastic casing.

3. Measure a length of white elastic to fit child around chest at underarms plus 2 in (5 cm). Thread elastic through opening. Sew ends together. Sew opening closed. Turn up hem and stitch (f). Sew lace along bottom and top edges if desired.

4. Sew 2 pieces of white ribbon to front and back top edges for shoulder straps (g). Press. Child should wear a white blouse under this top.

To Make Head Piece

1. Cover a plastic headband with a piece of the white material or ribbon (h). Sew lace to the edges of the covered headband if desired (i).

2. Use 1 yd (1 m) of stiff white tulle to make the veil (j). The material is folded into 2 or 3 layers when you buy it. Unfold and gather by running a needle with coarse thread knotted at one end in and out across the top of the material. Gather material until it fits the length of the top of the headband (k). Bind thread.

3. Sew gathered edge of veil to top of headband (k).

4. The child may carry a bouquet of artificial flowers.

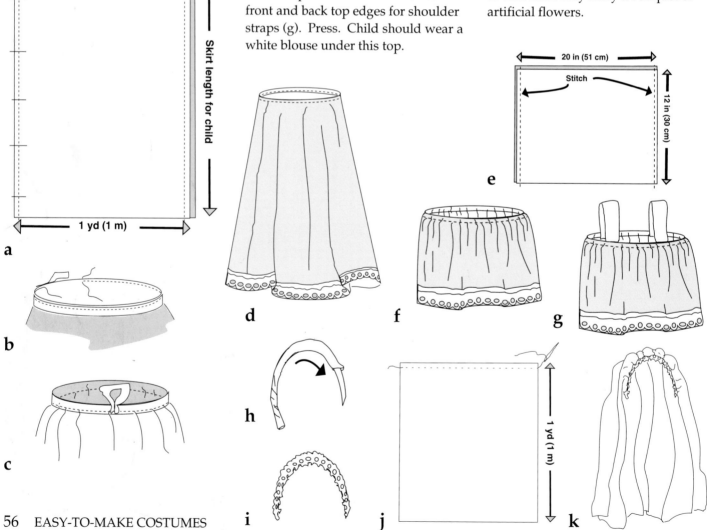

Reindeer

Materials

4-in (10-cm) -thick foam
small bell
red ribbon
paint

Costume is assembled on a brown track suit. Red reindeer nose optional.

To Make Antlers

1. Draw an antler pattern 12 in (30 cm) long on a piece of paper. Cut out.

2. Lay the pattern on 4-in (10-cm) thick foam and trace around it with a marker (a). Draw 2 antler shapes.

3. Cut around the shapes with a sharp utility knife. Shape the antler with the knife so that the prongs are about 1 in (2.5 cm) thick but angled in different directions, as shown (b).

4. From the scraps, cut out more prongs. Cut the base of the prongs at an angle and attach to the side of the main antler, using 5-minute epoxy (c).

To Make Ears

1. From scraps of foam, cut out 2 ears 5 in (12.5 cm) long and 3 in (7.5 cm) wide, as shown (d).

2. Cut out a piece of cardboard 8 in (20 cm) long and 4 in (10 cm) wide, oval shaped (e). With 5-minute epoxy, glue the antlers in the center and the ears at the ends, as shown (f).

3. Poke 2 holes in each end of the cardboard. Thread yarn or ribbon through the holes and glue in place, leaving enough ribbon hanging to tie under the chin (f).

4. Paint the cardboard and the ears brown and the antlers grey. Use bobby pins to secure to hair if necessary.

To Make Hooves

See **Lamb** costume instructions p 23.

To Make Collar

1. From scraps of foam, cut a strip 1 in (2.5 cm) wide and 15 in (28 cm) long (g).

2. Paint red and allow to dry.

3. Sew a bell at the center and a piece of ribbon 6 in (15 cm) long to each end to tie (h).

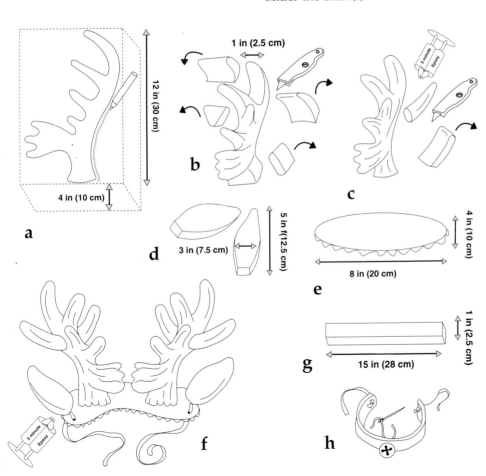

A & F

Fruit Basket

1. **Make Basic Cylinder A** p 8. Be sure the rippled side of the cardboard is turned outward (a).

To Make Handle

1. Cut 2 pieces of cardboard each 6 in (15 cm) wide and 1 yd (1 m) long (measure the length **across** the ripples).

2. Glue these 2 pieces of cardboard together, ripples on the outside (b).

3. Glue and staple the ends of the cardboard to the sides of the cylinder to form a handle by attaching one end of the handle in front of arm opening and attaching the other end of the handle on the other side of the cylinder behind the arm opening, as shown (c). The handle will arch over the child's head (see photo).

4. Paint a woven design on the cylinder and handle with brown paint (d).

5. Cut out leaves from green construction paper (e). Glue these around the top edge of the cylinder (see h).

6. Curl green pipe cleaners around your finger to make corkscrew shapes. These are tendrils (f). Poke end of pipe cleaner into top edge of cylinder.

7. Tie string to purchased artificial fruit and attach to the top edge of the cylinder by poking pairs of holes through the cardboard and tying the string on the inside of cylinder (g) (h).

To Make Hat

1. **Make Basic Bowl Hat F** p 14 (no brim).

2. Tightly roll up a piece of paper 3 in (7 cm) wide and 12 in (30 cm) long. Roll from the short end and tape (i).

3. Cut out a leaf from green paper (j).

4. Glue leaf to bottom of roll. Glue this end of the roll to the center of the top of the hat, as shown (k). Tape in place until dry. This is a stem.

5. Fold a green pipe cleaner in half (l). Roll the folded end of the pipe cleaner into a tight ball, leaving about 2 in (5 cm) straight. Bend over 1/2 in (1 cm) of the straight end (l). Glue this end to the side of the hat to make a worm (m).

6. Paint the hat yellow with a brown stem, to resemble an apple. You may paint the child's face to match the hat.

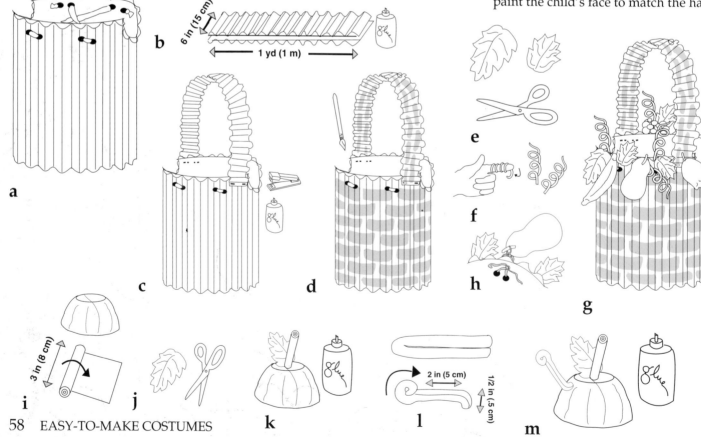

B

Sandwich

1. Make Basic Sandwich Board B
p 10, but substitute 1-in (2.5-cm) -thick foam 3 ft (1 m) square for the cardboard (a). **Do not punch holes** for ribbon.

2. With a brown felt marker draw the shape of a slice of bread on each piece of foam and cut out. Color the edge of the slice brown and draw brown and yellow circles and curls on the surface of the foam to resemble the texture of bread, as shown (a).

3. On flat cardboard draw rectangles with wavy edges and half circles, as shown (b). Make these about 12 in (30 cm) long and 8 in (20 cm) wide.

4. Paint the rectangles brown, red, and white to resemble bacon and the half circles red and yellow to resemble tomato slices.

5. Place front slice of bread face down and arrange the bacon and tomato slices around the edges (c).

6. Cut green crepe paper into pieces about 24 in (60 cm) long and 12 in (30 cm) wide. Bunch the paper along one side (d), to resemble leaves of lettuce.

7. With 5-minute epoxy, glue the bacon, lettuce, and tomato pieces around front slice so that they extend past the edges of the bread, as shown (e).

8. When the glue is set, attach the ribbons to the inside of the back foam board using 5-minute epoxy. Cross ribbon at back and glue ends to inside front of sandwich, as shown (c).

d

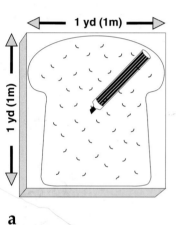

a

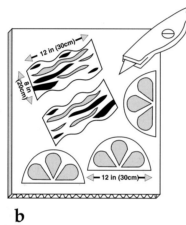

b

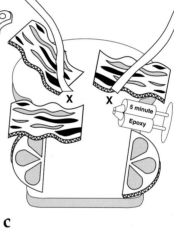

c

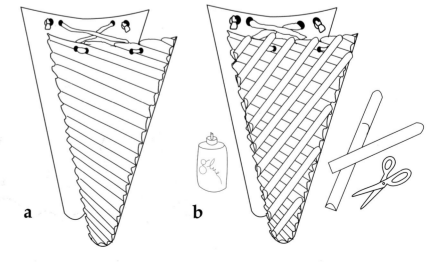

e

B

Ice-Cream Cone

1. Make Basic Sandwich Board B
p 10 using stiff corrugated cardboard. Cut the back and front of the board each in a cone shape.

2. Cut strips of cardboard the width of a single ripple. Glue these strips, ripple side up, across the surface of the cone, as shown (b).

a

b

Ice-Cream Cone Costume continued.
To Make Ice-Cream Head Piece

1. Select a paper bag to fit over the child's head. Cut a hole in the front for the child's face (c).

2. Use about 2 yds (2 m) polyester pillow stuffing to cover the paper bag.

3. Mix about 2 quarts (.5 l) of very thin poster paint the color of your favorite ice-cream flavor.

4. Dip the stuffing in this paint and wring most of the paint out again, leaving the stuffing tinted. Hang up the stuffing so it can drip dry. Use lots of newspapers to catch the excess paint. Dry overnight.

5. When dry, spread glue on the outside of the paper bag and wrap the stuffing around it (d). Fold the excess around the bottom edge and staple in place. Make sure the ends of the staples are on the outside of the bag, as shown (e).

6. Make 2 cuts in the stuffing over the face hole (f). Fold the excess stuffing inward and staple in the same way (g).

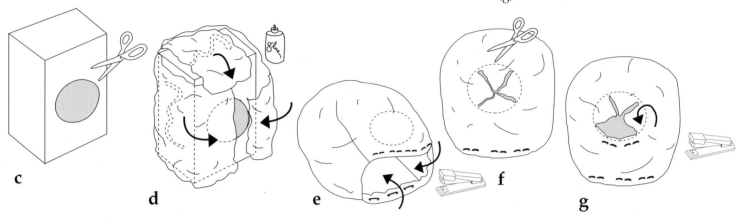

c

d

e

f

g

Use basic techniques A & G

Lollipop

1. **Make Basic Cylinder A** p 8 with armholes. Be sure the smooth side of the cardboard faces outward (a). Leave the cylinder unpainted to resemble a lollipop stick.

To Make Head Piece

1. **Make Basic Cylinder Hat G** p 15 (b).

2. Cut a circle from rippled cardboard 21 in (53 cm) in diameter (c).

3. Trace a smaller circle 8 in (20 cm) in diameter in the middle of this large circle. Cut out the smaller circle, leaving a ring (d), to frame face.

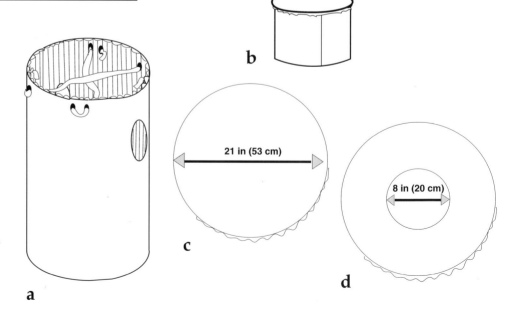

b

21 in (53 cm)

c

8 in (20 cm)

d

a

Lollipop Costume continued.

4. Cut a half circle 21 in (53 cm) wide at the base (e).

5. Spread glue over the front of the hat cylinder (f) and attach the rippled side of the ring to it (g). Place the ring so that the ripples are vertical, and the child can see through the hole in the middle.

6. Turn the hat over and spread glue over the back of the cylinder (h). Spread glue over the inside edges of the sides of the half circle (NOT the bottom) (i).

7. Attach the rippled side of the half circle to the back so that the curve is at the top, as shown (i), and press the sides of the half circle and the ring together, as shown (j). Tape in place until the glue dries.

8. Lay another piece of rippled cardboard flat, rippled side up. This piece must be large enough to cover the top of the hat (k).

9. Spread glue over the top edges of the hat and place the hat upside down on the flat cardboard, as shown (k). Tape in place. When the glue is dry, trim off excess cardboard, as shown (l).

10. On smooth cardboard, draw the letters for "LOLLIPOP." Make the letters 3 in (8 cm) high (m). Cut out. Glue these around the ring of the hat (n).

11. Paint the hat the color of your favorite lollipop. Paint the letters a slightly lighter shade of the same color by adding a bit of white paint to the color, so that the letters can be seen.

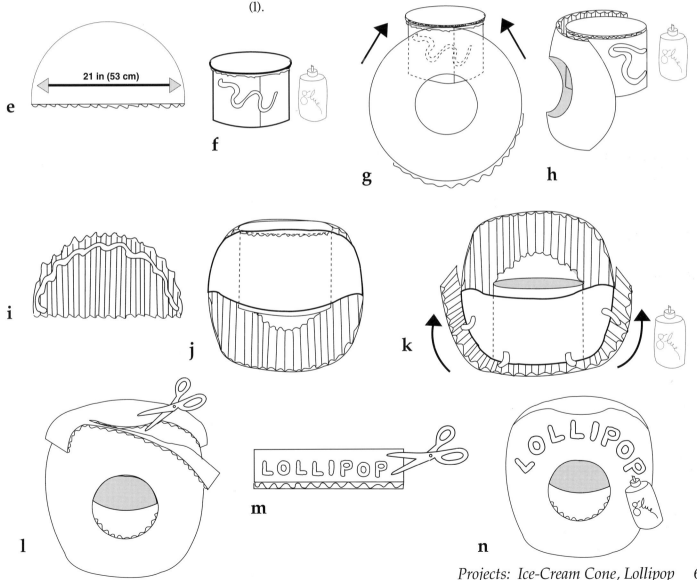

e   21 in (53 cm)

f

g

h

i

j

k

l

m   LOLLIPOP

n   LOLLIPOP

Spanish Dancer

Materials

3 yds (3 m) red cotton

elastic

bias tape 1 in (2.5 cm) wide

red, white, black ruffled trimming or lace

1/2 yd (.5 m) black lace remnant

1 yd (1 m) red cellophane ribbon 4 in (10 cm) wide and small hair comb

colored paper or purchased fan

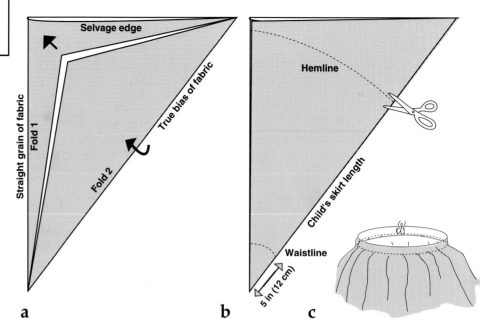

a   b   c

To Make Skirt

1. Fold red cotton in half (fold 1) and then diagonally (fold 2), as shown (a). Measure down 5 in (12 cm) from point as shown and cut waist. Measure the length of your child and mark off from waist on each side and center. Allow 2 in (5 cm) extra for hem and elastic seams. Draw a line to join points and cut along this line (b). This will give a very flared skirt.

2. Stitch side seams, right sides of fabric together. Press and turn.

3. Sew bias tape to waist on right side. Fold over to inside and stitch. This is the elastic casing. Measure child's waist and cut elastic to correct size, allowing for overlap to sew together. Thread elastic through casing (c). Sew ends together. Sew openings closed.

4. Sew red ruffle trimming to bottom of skirt (*see* photograph). Be sure to adjust length. Sew white ruffles and black lace around skirt to suit your taste.

Spanish Dancer Costume continued.

To Make Bolero

1. **Make Basic Vest E** p 14 from 1/2 yd (.5 m) black lace. See instructions for Ballerina, p 33.

To Make Hair Bow

1. Fold ribbon into loops for a bow, as shown (e). Staple to hold in place. Glue to a comb (f). Loop bow will stand up at back of child's head. Velvet bow may be worn as well.

To Make Paper Fan

1. Cut a strip of heavy colored paper 15 in (38 cm) long and 12 in (30 cm) wide. Fold from short side.

2. Make accordian pleating by folding back and forth (not over and over) until the paper is used up (g).

3. Staple one end, as shown (h). Spread out the other end. Decorate with glitter, ribbons, and lace, if desired.

Complete the costume with red leotards, red turtleneck, red ballet slippers, jewelry, and black fringed scarf tied at hips.

d

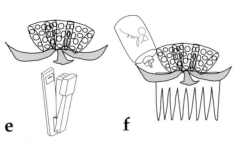

e   f

15 in (38 cm)

12 in (30 cm)

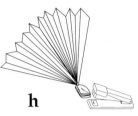

g   h

Use basic techniques

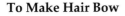

Tea Pot

1. **Make Basic Cylinder A** p 8 with armholes. Be sure the smooth side of the cardboard faces outward. This is the tea pot body (a).

To Make Spout

1. Cut a piece of cardboard 12 in (30 cm) wide and 16 in (40 cm) long, measuring the length **across** the ripples (b).

2. Roll the cardboard into a cylinder and secure with double-sided tape or glue (c).

3. With a sharp knife, cut one end of the cylinder at a steep angle (d).

4. Place this angled end against a piece of smooth cardboard and trace around it (e). Cut out and glue in place to the end of the spout cylinder (f).

5. When dry, glue the covered end of the spout cylinder to the front of the tea pot body cylinder, pointing spout upward, as shown (g). Hold or tape in place until the glue dries.

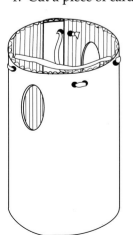

a

12 in (30 cm)

16 in (40 cm)

b

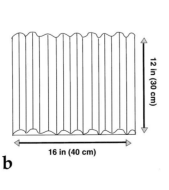

c

d

e   f

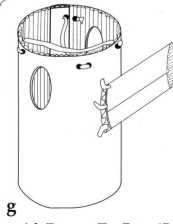

g

Tea Pot Costume continued.
To Make Handle

1. Draw a handle shape on smooth cardboard. Make sure the height of the handle is less than the height of the body cylinder. Draw the handle 2 in (5 cm) wide, as shown (h). Make 2 identical shapes. Cut out.

2. Cut a length of rippled cardboard 3 in (7 cm) wide and long enough to fit around the outside curve of the handle (i). Measure and cut the length **across** the ripples.

3. Lay the cardboard strip flat, rippled side up. Place a yardstick on the strip along the long edge, 1/2 in (1 cm) from the edge. Draw a sharp knife along the ruler, scoring the ripples but not cutting completely through the cardboard, as shown (j).

4. Pull off the rippled layer of paper, leaving the flat layer of paper along the outside edge beneath it, as shown (k). Repeat procedure on opposite edge of cardboard strip, as shown (l).

5. Make 1/2 in (1 cm) cuts all along these flat strip edges of paper along both sides of the long rippled strip, as shown (l).

6. Spread glue along the flat strip edges of paper on each side of the center rippled strip (m).

7. Place the outside edge of the handle shape on the glued paper so that the side of the handle is against the cut edges of the center ripples, and the handle and rippled strip are at right angles, as shown (n).

8. Fold the flat glued strip of paper over and onto the handle shape, as shown (o). Tape in place if necessary.

9. Repeat this procedure on the other side of the rippled strip with the second handle shape, as shown (p).

10. Cut another rippled strip of cardboard long enough to fit around the inside edge of the handle and across the ends. Remove 1/2 in (1 cm) from each side, as before.

11. Glue this second piece to one end of the handle and continue around the inside curve of the handle, as shown (q). Tape in place if necessary.

12. When the handle is completely dry, glue it to the back of the cylinder. Tape in place until the glue dries (r).

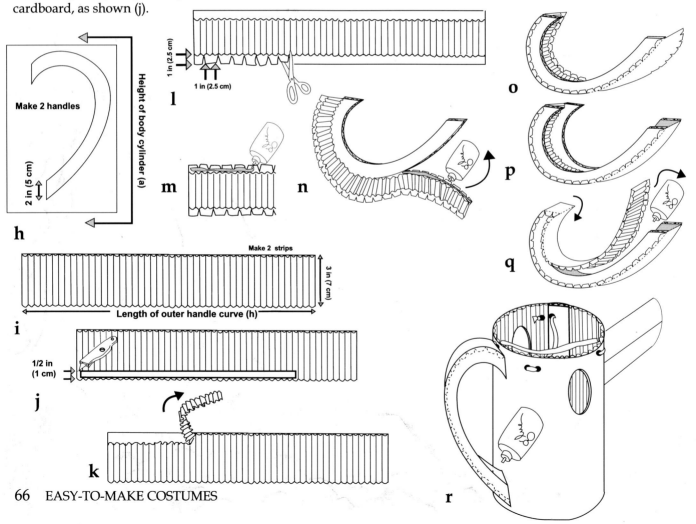

Make 2 handles

Height of body cylinder (a)

2 in (5 cm)

1 in (2.5 cm)

1 in (2.5 cm)

h

l

m

n

o

p

q

Make 2 strips

3 in (7 cm)

Length of outer handle curve (h)

i

1/2 in (1 cm)

j

k

r

Tea Pot Costume continued.
To Make Tea Pot Lid

1. **Make Basic Cylinder Hat G** p 15 (s).

2. Cut a circle 18 in (46 cm) in diameter and glue to the top of the cylinder (t), to resemble a tea pot lid.

3. Make a smaller cylinder for the handle of the lid. Cut a strip of rippled cardboard 9 in (23 cm) long and 3 in (8 cm) wide, measuring the length **across** the ripples. Roll into cylinder and glue or tape (u).

4. Place the end of the cylinder on another piece of cardboard and trace around it to make a circle the same size (v). Cut out and glue to one end of the cylinder (w). Glue the other end of the cylinder to the center of the large circle on the top of the hat (x).

5. Paint the tea pot with flowers to resemble a fancy china pot.

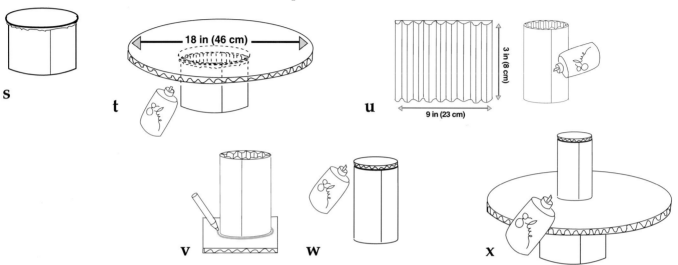

No basic technique required.
Instructions complete on pp 68-69

Old-Fashioned Lady

Materials
2 lengths of pink fabric for dress (measure the length from shoulder to hem)
1 yd (1 m) of sparkling pink lacy fabric for overskirt
3/4 yd (.7 m) silver fabric for sleeves
velcro
3 yds (3 m) of 4-in (10-cm) -wide satin ribbon for sash
6 yds (6 m) of 4-in (10-cm) -wide pink lace for trim and hat ties
purchased straw hat

artificial flowers
1 yd (1 m) pink folded bias tape
  or ribbon
unfolded bias tape

To Make Dress

1. Use the grid (a), adjust size, cut out pattern and place on pink fabric. Cut out. Stitch shoulder seams together (1 & 2) on wrong side. Stitch back

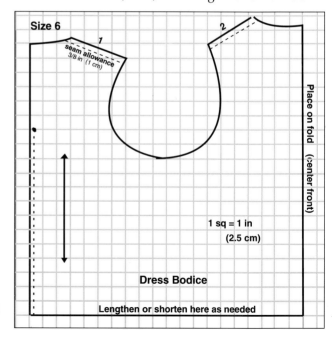

Size 6
seam allowance
3/8 in (1 cm)
1
2
Place on fold (center front)
1 sq = 1 in
(2.5 cm)
Dress Bodice
Lengthen or shorten here as needed

a

Old-Fashioned Lady Costume continued. seam to dot. Turn under back opening seam allowance and stitch. Sew velcro on back opening. Turn under neck edges and stitch.

2. Use grid (b) for sleeve. Cut out pattern and place on silver fabric. Cut out 2. Stitch 1 in (2.5 cm) wide bias tape to right side of sleeve edge. Turn under and stitch. This is the elastic casing. Tack lace to sleeve edge. Stitch sleeve sides together (3 & 4), and lace ends. Gather top of sleeve (c) to fit bodice armhole. Stitch in

armhole (d). Thread elastic through casing. Measure on child's arm. Sew ends.

To Make Skirt and Overskirt

1. Measure child from waist to floor, add 2 in (5 cm) for hem and cut off this length of pink fabric (make width as wide as fabric). Make 2. Stitch side seams. Stitch 1 in (2.5 cm) wide tape to right side of waist. Turn to inside and stitch for elastic casing. Thread through elastic. Measure child's waist size and cut off elastic. Sew ends.

Adjust length of skirt hem. Stitch (e).

2. Hem 3 sides of sparkling pink fabric. Gather unhemmed end of fabric. Adjust to child's waist size and stitch folded bias tape over gathers (f). Hem ends. Sew piece of narrow ribbon at each end for ties. Sew wide lace or ruffle to bottom. This is the overskirt (g). Make a silver rosette by folding over scraps of silver fabric and sewing. Tack to overskirt (*see* photo).

3. Make a ribbon sash (h) to tie around waist with large bow at back. Sash can be trimmed with silver fabric, if desired.

6. Add artificial flowers to front of hat. Drape 2 yds (2 m) of wide lace over hat and tie under chin (i). Child may carry artificial flowers.

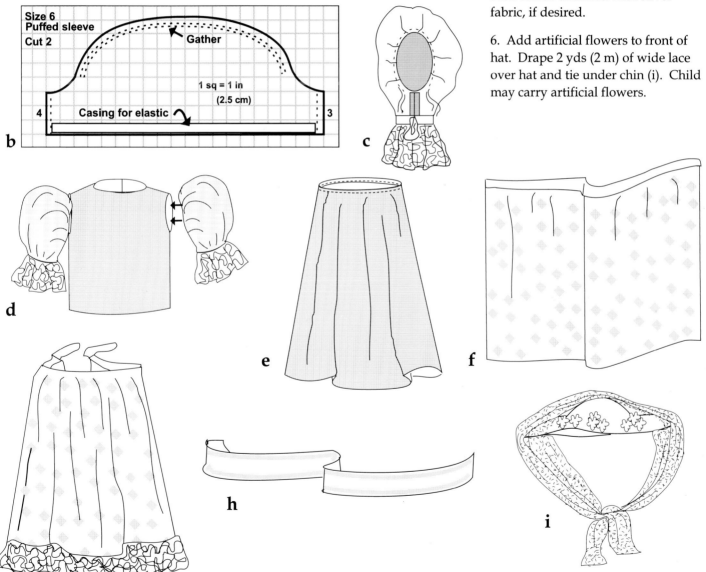

H

Clown

Materials
purchased clown nose
1 yd (1 m) colorful fabric
**1 skein each red, yellow, blue thick
  yarn**
velcro
1 sheet of pliable cardboard
**unfolded bias tape and folded bias
  tape**
Costume assembled on a multicolored
track suit.

To Make Hat

1. **Make Basic Cone Hat H** p 15 using
lightweight cardboard.

2. Wrap fabric around hat to cover it
(a). Cut off excess fabric to use for
collar, wrist, and ankle ruffles.

3. Glue fabric to hat. Fold over edges
and glue. Allow to dry.

4. Finish by gluing 3 pom-poms (one
of each color) down the front of the
hat, as shown (b).

To Make Pom-Poms

1. Make several pom-poms with
   each color of yarn. Wind end of
yarn about 20 times (more or less for
fluffiness of pom-pom) around a piece
of cardboard 6 in (15 cm) long, as
shown (c).

2. Slide yarn off cardboard carefully
and wrap yarn end tightly around
middle of yarn. Cut off yarn end and
tie securely with one cut end (d). Cut
ends of yarn (e).

3. Fluff out pom-pom and tie or sew
to project (*see* b). NOTE: Size of pom-
pom can be changed by varying the
width of the piece of cardboard.

To Make Wrist and Ankle Ruffles

1. Use the leftover fabric from the
clown hat. Measure and cut out 2
strips 6 in (15 cm) wide and 12 in (30
cm) long for the wrist ruffles (f).

2. Measure and cut out 2 more strips
6 in (15 cm) wide and 14 in (35 cm)
long for the ankle ruffles (f).

3. Sew tape on inside middle of each
strip for elastic casing. Sew short ends
of each strip together leaving an
opening to insert the elastic (g).

4. If fabric frays, hem the edges by
turning under 1/4 in (.6 cm) or serge
with an overlock machine.

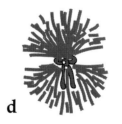

c

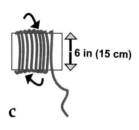

d

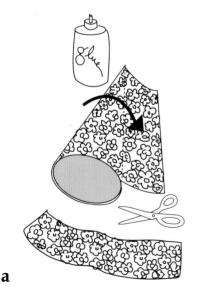

a

b

e

Clown Costume continued.

5. Measure the child's wrist and ankle and cut elastic to fit loosely. Thread elastic through casing. Sew ends together and sew casing closed (g).

6. Attach a pom-pom to the front of each ruffle mixing and matching colors, as desired (h).

To Make Collar

1. Cut a strip of fabric 30 in (76 cm) long and 6 in (15 cm) wide on the bias, as shown (i). Use same fabric or contrast, as desired.

2. If fabric frays, turn under hem on short ends and stitch or serge with overlock machine.

3. Stitch velcro on these ends to close collar (j).

4. Turn under seam allowance on one length and stitch.

5. Make small running stitches on unhemmed side and pull thread to gather material (k). Adjust length to fit around child's neck.

6. Pin and stitch folded bias tape over this gathered side to finish (k).

7. Paint child's face, if desired. Child can wear a red plush clown nose.

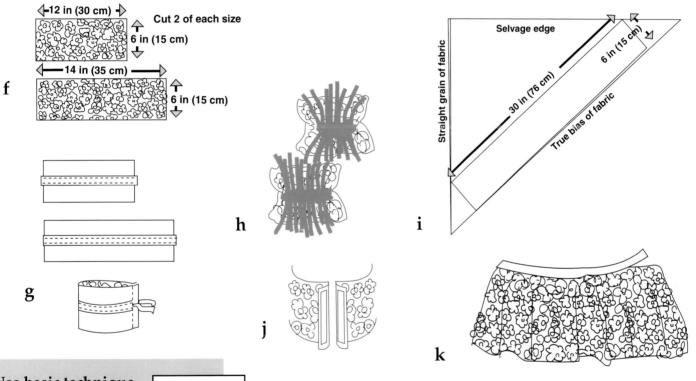

Use basic technique

A

Daisy

1. **Make Basic Cylinder A** p 8. Paint green.

2. Cut out leaf shapes from rippled cardboard **across** the ripples, as shown (a). Paint green and glue to the cylinder (b).

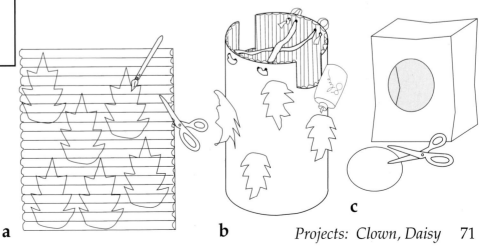

Daisy Costume continued.

To Make Hat

1. Select a paper bag to fit over the child's head. Cut a hole in the center of the front for the child's face (c).

2. Cut out petals from rippled cardboard. Cut some across the ripples, and some in the same direction as the ripples, as shown (d).

3. One petal at a time, spread glue over the rippled side. Curl the petal along the ripples and join it to another piece of rippled cardboard by fitting the ripples together, as shown (e), so that the petal will hold its shape. The ripples will not fit together evenly, but will skip a section here and there. This is what holds the petal in a curve.

4. Tape together until the glue dries (f).

3. When dry arrange the petals around the hole in the paper bag and glue in place (g).

6. Cut pieces of paper 1 in (2.5 cm) wide and 2 in (5 cm) long. Fringe the pieces along the long side, as shown (h), and paint yellow. Glue in place around the hole (i).

7. Paint the paper bag green and paint the petals white.

8. Decorate the child's face with yellow face paint for the center of the flower.

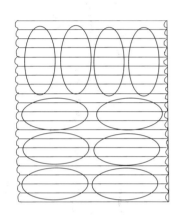

d

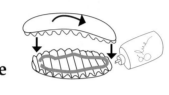

e

f

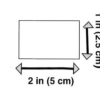

1 in (2.5 cm)

2 in (5 cm)

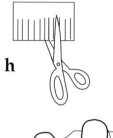

h

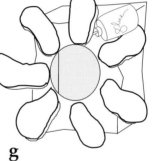

g

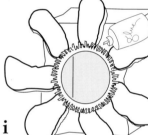

i

C&G

Box of Crayons

1. **Make Basic Box C** p 11. Use a box that fits the child and that is much wider than it is deep. Shoulder straps are not required.

2. Cut off the flaps at the bottom and on **3 sides only** at the top leaving one of the flaps of the wider side on the top of the box, as shown (a).

3. Fold it back to resemble the top of a crayon box (b). Paint to resemble a crayon box. Cut out holes for hands.

a

Crayons

b

Box of Crayons Costume continued.
To Make Hat

1. **Make Basic Cylinder Hat G** p 15 (c).

2. Make the cylinder to fit the child's head. Do not cut a cardboard circle for the top. Instead, glue 2 sheets of paper together and roll into a paper cone (d). Make the opening of the cone so that it is large enough to fit over the cylinder. Glue or tape the cone (e).

3. Make 1 in (2.5 cm) cuts around the opening of the cone, as shown (f). Spread glue around the inside edge of this cut edge (g).

4. Press the opening of the cone over the cylinder and press the glued tabs against the outside of the cone (h).

5. Cut a strip of paper 2 in (5 cm) wide and long enough to go around the cylinder. Spread glue on one side of the paper strip and wrap around the cylinder, covering the tabs, as shown (i).

6. Paint a bright color. You may paint the child's face to match the color of the crayon hat.

7. Make 2 more hats the same way. Make them small enough to fit inside the box, as shown (j). Paint bright colors. When dry, glue one on each side of the box to resemble other crayons.

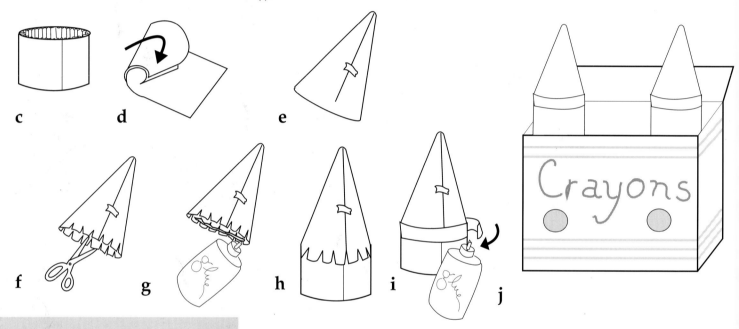

c   d   e

f   g   h   i   j

A & G

Tree

1. **Make Basic Cylinder A** p 8 with armholes. Be sure the rippled side of the cardboard is turned outward. This is the trunk of the tree (a).

2. Cut different lengths of cardboard up to 18 in (46 cm) long and 3 in (7 cm) wide, measuring the length along the ripples (b). Roll the pieces of

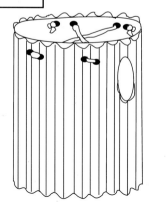

a

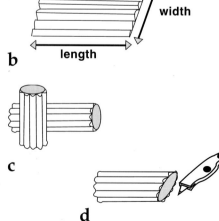

b

width

length

c

d

Tree Costume continued.

cardboard into tubes to make many branches. Secure tubes with double-sided tape or with glue (c).

3. With a sharp knife, cut one end of each tube at an angle, as shown (d).

4. Glue the largest branches to the outside of the cylinder. Attach the angled end of each tube around the top edge so that the branches stick up and away from the cylinder, as shown (e). Secure with tape until dry.

5. Attach smaller branches to the large branches in the same way (f). You can also attach small thin pieces of flat cardboard to the branches for twigs.

6. Paint the cylinder and branches brown and grey to resemble tree bark.

7. Cut many leaves from green paper or white paper painted green and glue these to the branches (g).

To Make Hat

1. **Make Basic Cylinder Hat G** p 15. Be sure the rippled side of the cardboard is turned outward. Cut a small circle of cardboard the same size as the cylinder and glue to one end of the cylinder, for the top (h).

3. Make a few small branches in the same way as for the tree cylinder, and glue to the outside of the hat cylinder (i).

4. Cut out green leaves and attach to the hat "branches" (j).

5. Cut many small pieces of flat cardboard, approximately 3 in (7 cm) long and 1/2 in (1 cm) wide. Arrange these in a circle around the top of the hat and glue in place to form a bird's nest (k).

6. Paint to match the tree. Place purchased small toy birds in the nest.

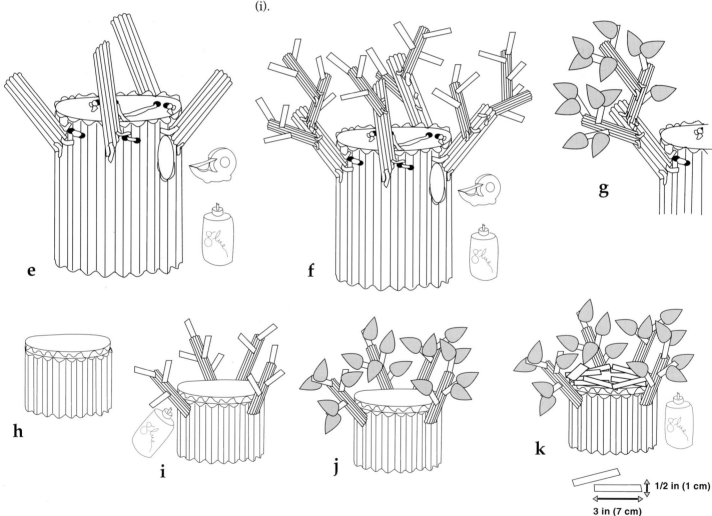

1/2 in (1 cm)

3 in (7 cm)

B

King of Hearts

1. **Make Basic Sandwich Board B** p 10 but substitute 1-in (2.5-cm) -thick foam for cardboard, and use felt markers to color the foam. **Do not punch holes for ribbons** (a).

2. Use a face card from a deck of cards as a pattern example. Draw card pattern on tissue paper. Draw the faces as large as the child's face (b). Transfer the pattern to the foam (c). Trace around the oblong card shape, as shown (c), cut this off pattern, return to foam and trace with a red or black marker around oblong on foam.

3. Cut out around the figure on the paper pattern (d).

4. Position the paper pattern on the foam again, and continue to trace around it (d).

5. Draw the 2 faces on the foam, but **draw details on one face only**. Cut a hole for the child's face in the other face (e).

6. On the other half of the sandwich, draw a geometric pattern to resemble the back of a card (f).

7. Fit the child's face through the face shape hole in the card, and mark the shoulder height at the back of the front card (g). Attach the ribbons to the card at the height marked with 5-minute epoxy. Cross the ribbons and attach to the inside of the back card with 5-minute epoxy.

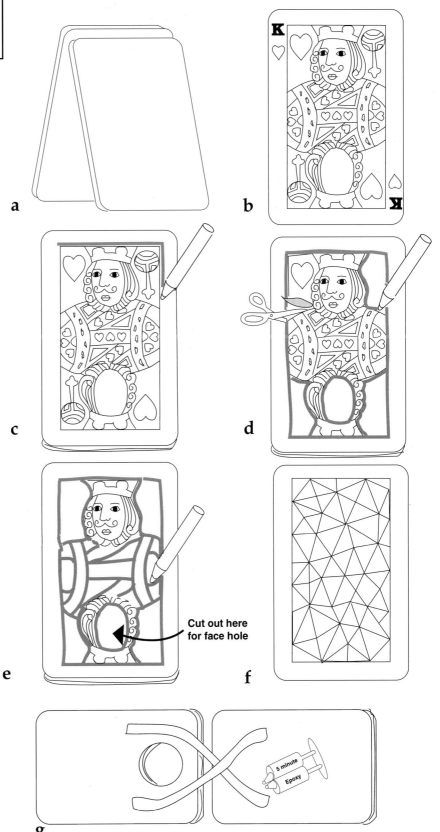

a

b

c

d

e

Cut out here for face hole

f

g

B&F&G

Alarm Clock

1. Make Basic Sandwich Board B
p 10 using a circle with a diameter of 30 in (75 cm) (a).

2. From scraps of smooth cardboard, cut out the numbers and hands for a clock face and glue in place on the front board (b).

3. From scraps of smooth cardboard, cut out small circles of various sizes. Cut out notches, as shown (c), to resemble cogs and gears.

4. From rippled cardboard, make 3 small cylinders 4 in (10 cm) long and 2 in (5 cm) in diameter (d). Place the ends of the cylinders on smooth cardboard and trace around them. Cut out each circle and glue to the ends of the cylinders (e). Save one cylinder for a key.

5. Use the leftover cylinder for the key. Draw an "8" shape 6 in (15 cm) long. Cut out the holes in the centers and cut around the "8", as shown (f). Make 2 notches in the top of the leftover cylinder and glue the key handle into the notches (g).

6. Glue the open ends of the cylinders, along with the "gears" and the "key" to the back board, as shown (h).

To Make Alarm Bells

1. **Make 2 Basic Bowl Hats F** p 14. Use a larger bowl for the mold than you would for a hat.

2. When dry and hard, cover outside surface with aluminum foil (i). Glue.

3. Make 2 cardboard cylinders from rippled cardboard. Make the cylinders 15 in (38 cm) long and 3 in (7.5 cm) in diameter (j).

4. Make 5 cuts in one end of each cylinder 2 in (5 cm) long (j). Bend each tab back and spread with glue. Press the glued tabs of one cylinder to the inside of one of the large paper

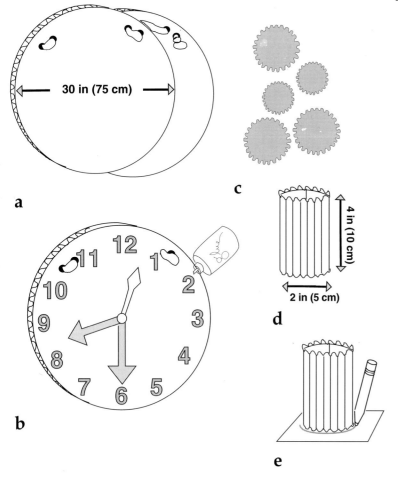

a

b

c

d

4 in (10 cm)

2 in (5 cm)

e

Alarm Clock Costume continued.
bowls (k). Repeat with the other cylinder and bowl. Tape in place.

5. When dry, flatten the other end of the cylinders. Glue and staple these ends to the back of the front board, as shown (l).

To Make Alarm Button Hat

1. **Make Basic Cylinder Hat G** p 15. Place smooth side of cardboard outward (m).

2. Make another cylinder 10 in (25 cm) long and 5 in (12 cm) in diameter (smooth side outward). Cut 2 circles to fit the ends of this cylinder and glue in place (n).

3. Lay this cylinder on the top of the hat, as shown (o), and glue and tape in place. Cover the hat with aluminum foil.

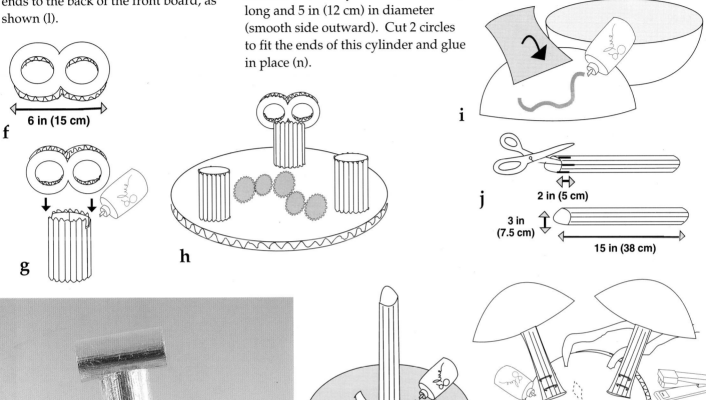

f

6 in (15 cm)

g

h

i

j

2 in (5 cm)

3 in (7.5 cm)

15 in (38 cm)

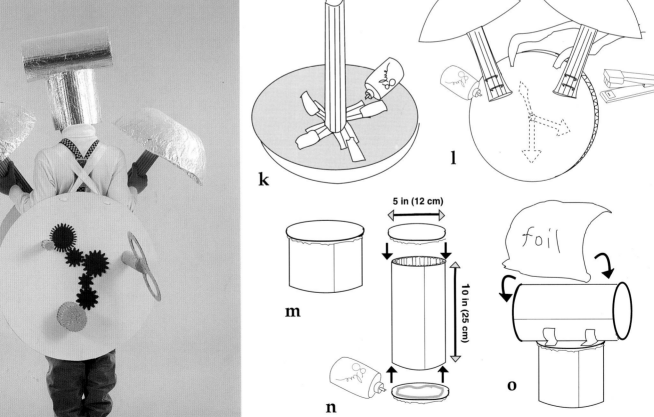

k

l

m

5 in (12 cm)

10 in (25 cm)

n

foil

o

INDEX

Note: photographs of costumes or props are listed in boldface and *italic*.